Praise for **One-Blo**

"A fascinating collection of pieces about my favorite neighborhood in Spokane."
—Jess Walter, National Book Award Finalist and *#1 New York Times* bestselling author of *Beautiful Ruins*

"Over the past two decades I have had a front row seat to watch the transformation of the Community Building Campus and to witness the ripples of positive impacts it has created. This book perfectly captures the long arc of local, grassroots, community-led change sparked by the Community Building, which has helped to make Spokane and Washington State a more just and equitable place for all."
—Senator Andy Billig, Washington State Senate Majority Leader

"This fascinating book puts Spokane on the progressive map. Cities across the country should envy a street given over to nonprofit causes, health food, and leading-edge entertainments. Twenty contributors outline the altruisms they could undertake thanks to the benefactor who bought the buildings so they could mount their little revolution in this once-gritty city."
—Paul Lindholdt, Washington State Book Award-winning author of *In Earshot of Water*

"Jim Sheehan's vision of creating space for a thriving community of advocates, visionaries, and changemakers was extraordinary. The story of how he brought that vision to life is an inspiring model for the rest of us who say we want to BE the change that we seek in the world. Grateful for his vision, the community of changemakers and impact they've had on Spokane."
—Regina Malveaux, Executive Director, Washington State Women's Commission

"The stories in this volume tie together a rich history of social innovation and economic development in a mid-size American city. The careful editing creates a robust set of stories about a dynamic ecosystem that should be on the bookshelves of developers, philanthropists, public servants, and citizens of growing cities."
—Michael Ebinger, Ph.D., MBA, former director of the WSU Center for Innovation, Spokane

"Sense of purpose enhanced by sense of place; this one-block revolution has become home to a community of good people and good organizations doing great things for our world. Led by the vision of one person, this is an example of values brought to life through action and multiplied by community. The Community Building Campus is inspiration for us all to join the movement to make our world a better place, one block at a time."

–Matt Santangelo, Executive Director of Spokane Hoopfest Association

"Having relocated to Spokane to be a part of the one-block revolution, I've witnessed firsthand the impact of that transformation on the entire city. Now it's time for all of us to expand the revolution into one that transforms communities across the United States, and this book is an essential guide for anyone who wants to do exactly that."

–Thomas Linzey, Senior Legal Counsel, Center for Democratic and Environmental Rights

"A great case study on place-based social change. It takes place in Washington State, but readers from anywhere will find the pages packed with lessons, cautionary tales, best practices, and inspiration."

–Jon Snyder, Outdoor Recreation and Economic Development Senior Policy Advisor to Gov. Jay Inslee

"'If these walls could talk' is a common refrain, but rarely do we get to hear what they would say. These reflections and stories describe a special place that has inspired and compelled me in my work to not just build places but community. *One-Block Revolution* allows the stories of these people and this place to spread, inspire, and challenge far beyond the block they originated."

–Lars Gilberts, AVP Community Development & Impact for Numerica Credit Union

"It's rare to get such an in-depth view of the rippling effects social purpose real estate has in a community. What a gift to hear from the multiple voices in *One-Block Revolution* that built this inclusive, welcoming community and continue building it, a collective and infinite legacy."

–Leena Waite, Consulting Coordinator for The Nonprofit Centers Network

"The Community Building pulses with its own energy and seemingly emits its own semiochemical that is intoxicating to anyone whose signals bend towards vision, creativity, humanity, social justice, leadership; i.e. community. *One-Block Revolution* is an inspiring read, not just about how one building cluster changed one mid-sized American city, but also about how many hearts, minds, and souls made it possible for so many people in Spokane to find themselves and their tribe and how those people collectively continue to do good for the world."

–Bart Mihailovich, Organizing Manager, U.S. Waterkeeper Alliance

"Having worked with Jim Sheehan and his team—many of whom have both lived and authored the provocative essays in *One-Block Revolution*—I've seen up close how this experiment in place-based intelligence and investment in relationships, culture, and collaboration have driven social innovation that endures. This radical approach to philanthropy rebalances power and creates the conditions for community-led change."

–Toby Herzlich, Founder, Biomimicry for Social Innovation

"It has been a joy, over the last twenty-plus years, to watch the Community Building Campus grow as a vibrant and inclusive district within the Spokane University District...and now, a joy to read about the people that made it happen."

–Juliet Sinisterra, CEO (interim), Spokane University District

"Don't be deceived. This book is not about a building. It is about creating the conditions that nurture possibility. Interwoven stories reveal the hopes and aspirations of an unlikely set of companions....This is the story of what's done when we want to do community building."

–Bob Stilger, Ph.D., Founder of NewStories

"*One-Block Revolution* invites everyone who is community-minded to join a worthy experiment that considers, 'What does it take for all of a community's residents to thrive for everyone?' For those of us trying to answer this question in our own communities, this book stirs the imagination, challenges status quo assumptions to community development, and offers helpful lessons learned."

–Mike Bontrager, Founder of Chatham Financial and Co-founder of Square Roots Collective

"Nearly fifty years ago, Jim Sheehan frequently and generously shared his world-vision with his friends. 'Sheehanisms' we called these sharings. Idealistic. Beyond reach. But the Fates smiled and Jim acted. In the perfectly titled, *One-Block Revolution*, the legacy of Jim's action is recorded. The essays include thoughtful tutorials on the role of leadership and philanthropy in promoting a just society—included, no doubt, as a clarion call to those with the means to act boldly and advance the revolution."

–Thomas Hillier, longtime Federal Public Defender

"*One-Block Revolution* is an informative, engaging, and must-read book for anyone who cares about social change and social justice. Each contributor was an active and distinctive participant in the two decades of Jim Sheehan's Community Building Campus, and each chapter, like pieces of a puzzle, adds its own shape and color to this Spokane adventure in Community Buildings and Building Community."

–Dr. C. Earl Leininger, Professor of Philosophy & Religion at Mars Hill University (retired)

"A great behind-the-scenes look at how intentional development can preserve a neighborhood's character, grow community, and advance social and environmental justice while still being an economic success. Spokane is fortunate to have this gem anchoring the east end of downtown."

–Sharon Smith, Trustee for the Smith-Barbieri Progressive Fund, A Charitable Foundation

"*One-Block Revolution* is truly a neverending story that extends far beyond two hundred pages, one-hundred-year-old brick walls, and Spokane's city limits. The passion, vision, and audacity of the people who helped contribute to the last twenty years of community building have been instrumental in inspiring others to not only reimagine Spokane, but reimagine our world. "

–Ryann Louie, Co-chair of APIC Spokane & Founder of Reimagine Spokane

"What an insightful and helpful look at the benefits, blessings, and profound struggles inherent in community building and collaboration. *One-Block Revolution* provides inspiration and guidance for individuals and organizations working to build equitable and healthy communities."

–Ryan Oelrich, Executive Director, Priority Spokane

"The Community Building is a great example on the spectrum of community shared space, and this book lifts up its vibrant story. It's also a call to action for real estate owners to put their buildings into community service—particularly around leaving a legacy of impact as we head into one of the greatest intergenerational wealth transfers in history of the United States."

–Saul Ettlin, Director of Consulting, Community Vision

"*One-Block Revolution* captures the nerve and verve of community building and the value of empowering the voices of ordinary people and turning those voices into action."

–Steve Maher, Director of Our Valley Our Future / Nuestro Valle Nuestro Futuro, Wenatchee

"Physical spaces – even, and maybe especially, those that are small in square footage – can be the spark and the home base that encourage us to act bravely, explore new ideas, and foster collective flourishing. *One-Block Revolution* is as engaging for those of us who have planted ourselves in this city and on this particular block as it will be for those seeking and building community anywhere."

–Breanne Durham, Washington Main Street Director, Washington Trust for Historic Preservation

"A shining example of how ordinary citizens have the power to improve the lives of fellow citizens with creativity, passion, and commitment. A great testament to the very American tradition of philanthropy."

–Beth Stipe, Executive Director, Community Foundation of North Central Washington

One-Block Revolution

One-Block Revolution

20 Years of Community Building

Edited by
Summer Hess

One-Block Revolution:
20 Years of Community Building

Edited by Summer Hess

Copyright © 2021 by Community Building Foundation

Book design by Kevin Breen
Cover illustration by Jacquelyn Barnes

ISBN: 978-1-7360127-5-8
Cataloging-in-Publication Data is available upon request

Manufactured in the United States of America

Published by Latah Books
Spokane, Washington
www.latahbooks.com

Summer Hess may be contacted at summer@sagestepsolutions.com

CONTENTS

Introduction

Community Building Is a Noun and a Verb

By Summer Hess

Soon after starting my job in 2013 as executive assistant to Jim Sheehan, founder of the Center for Justice and the Community Building Campus in Spokane, Washington, I returned to our office after lunch to a voice message from a Coca-Cola representative. He was calling about an old advertisement painted directly on the southwest corner of the Community Building and offered to have it restored, free of charge.

It seemed like a great idea to me. I was a newly minted MFA in nonfiction writing who felt a strong connection to the Spokane region and Eastern Washington University, where I had earned my degree. I felt the faded advertisements on early 20th-century brick evoked nostalgia for the early days of the Inland Empire. They spoke to a classic Spokane era, when industry boomed, when timber and minerals were trucked out by train and money flowed in, when buildings were so finely crafted each of them had a name. They also brightened and textured a city still creeping back from the shift out of downtown and into the suburbs. These advertisements, along with Art Deco flourishes on historic theaters and wide avenues planned during a period of abundance, made it easier to look past street-level parking garages and sparsely populated storefronts.

Like many mid-sized American cities, Spokane is also experiencing a reversal of this trend. Businesses are repopulating downtown, and people like me—born and raised thousands of miles away—are moving to the region for its high quality of life and education. If rapidly increasing property values are any indication, the city is changing quickly—at a slower pace than some residents would like, but at a rate that seems too sudden for others. As the density in downtown increases, Spokane has become more politically diverse. The Northwest Progressive Institute reports that the Clinton-Kaine ticket won the City of Spokane by eleven points in 2016, while Trump-Pence won Spokane County by nine. In 2020, Biden-Harris carried the city by seventeen points, while the county went Trump-Pence by four. Although this was an unusual election year, Spokane is representative of the national urban-rural divide, where higher population densities are shifting cities to be more progressive than their surroundings. The Community Building Campus (CBC) has served as the nerve center for planning, organizing, campaigning for, and accelerating this kind of progressive social change in the Spokane region.

But in 2013 I wasn't tuned into the political landscape of Spokane; I was just excited to share a mural restoration project with my boss. I had been hired part-time as his executive assistant, and all that I knew about my job was that I was supposed to answer his mail and manage his calendar, which took about two hours a week. I knew that his previous assistant had helped him with unique and seemingly unrelated projects, from staging a theatrical reading of *Love Letters* with his life partner, Mary, to serving as non-voting secretary for the Center for Justice board, to organizing an annual pop-up soccer camp for kids at a nearby park. I had no experience in theater, but I could participate in this small piece of historic preservation. Jim and his team had gutted and, wherever possible, restored six buildings on the same block of Main Avenue, and I perceived them as testaments to his commitment to historic architecture. Surely, he would be excited about the mural project, too.

Jim returned to his office after enjoying a cup of soup from the Saranac Pub on the first floor of the building next door, said hello, and sat behind the credenza for his afternoon scroll through *The Huffington Post*.

"I had an interesting voicemail come through," I said from my desk that peered out over Main Avenue, watching the lunch rush at the Main Market Co-op and Boots Bakery.

"Oh?" he asked, without looking up. He was dressed in his usual sweatshirt and track pants, which he had worn to a personal training session earlier that day. I told him about the Coca-Cola rep and his offer.

Still scrolling, his immediate response was, "Tell them they can restore the advertisement when they stop using love and happiness to sell a f---ing product."

His tone was not angry, but it was clear. So was the fact that I was not working for your average developer or philanthropist. This guy saw a lot more at stake in the world than his profit margins or the public visibility of his family's foundation. Even in something as benign as peeling paint, he saw the manipulative clutches of capitalism clashing with a higher good. I realized how complex my position as an executive assistant was going to be. Should I deliver his opinion verbatim? Should I spare the rep who was obviously a cog in the structure of a global corporation? Should I temper the language and communicate the message?

In that particular moment, I took no action. Telling the Coca-Cola rep about Jim's stance on capitalism did not seem necessary. It was around that time I printed off the Community Building's mission statement and taped it to my computer: "To host, inspire, and catalyze social change in the Spokane region." I had no idea how an executive assistant could be an agent for change, but I kept the mantra in mind as I sorted out my place among the staff who managed the buildings that hosted more than forty nonprofits, small businesses, and state politicians. I did not know what my role was yet, but I knew the CBC was a place I wanted to be.

This was the most dynamic block in the city, and not just for social enterprises and nonprofits. Several other committed business owners operated eateries and unique shops. There was a constant refresh of energy on the block as students flowed in and out of bars and cafés, and activists trotted back and forth from public meetings or one-on-one brainstorming sessions. The CBC also included a two-screen independent movie theater, an art gallery, a food co-op, and a large multi-vendor space called the Saranac Commons. People who knew nothing of social justice movements happening above the ground floor came to eat, drink, and participate in diverse aspects of public life together.

Over time, I began to experience what Jim and the people he worked with were after. I learned that, as a career public defender, Jim understood how inequality threatens the livelihoods—and at times, the lives—of people in our communities, but there was little he could do from within the system to effect change. Then his aunt left him an unexpected windfall inheritance, giving him the chance to make the difference he had always dreamed of. That's when he began to buy, restore, and repurpose historic buildings on Main Avenue as living, sustainable monuments to social justice. He invited local citizens and community leaders to leverage his personal wealth as a collective resource and invested in the conditions for social innovation. Most importantly, I believe, he took advantage of a rare opportunity to stop treading water in the current system and to start asking, what's possible?

Eight years after the Coca-Cola incident, and after several evolutions of my role and responsibilities, I am still the messenger, attempting to name and outline what can happen when resources and space are dedicated not just to a specific project, but a higher purpose. In the process of curating and editing this anthology, I find myself working anew toward that mission I had taped to my computer: to host, inspire, and catalyze social change, this time through the voices and stories of people who built and shaped this vision.

My conclusion after several years of interviewing people about the CBC for this project is that it's more than a socially minded co-working space or small business accelerator. It is a countercultural, social, and architectural experiment that offers institutional infrastructure and support that is normally out of reach for small, grassroots organizations. It bolsters their connectivity, visibility, and collective power. It empowers people who don't have a voice and advances systemic social change at the local level. It provides fertile ground for future leaders, the young people who intern or find summer work here, who soak up the ethos of community building.

The CBC has served as an incubator and launch pad for twenty years of campaigns, coalitions, and conversations that have influenced policies, elections, and cultural shifts. In the following pages, twenty leaders and collaborators report on these two decades of growth and experimentation. They provide insights on how real estate can be repurposed as a dynamic hub for changemakers, and reimagined to generate alternative assets such as health, equality, beauty, justice, and love. Turn to words penned by Breean Beggs and Patty Gates for more on long-term impacts nurtured by the CBC. As they note, all of this is nearly impossible to quantify, but our hope is that the reach can be better understood if we share some of the stories of what happened here.

Today, I believe the CBC is a leading place-based model for addressing systemic inequalities. It was conceptualized for—and especially, with—the people, and demonstrates a new trend in philanthropy, as Nina Simons details later in these pages. At the CBC, citizens engage in the activation of private resources, demonstrating that the radical shift from building wealth to building the local community is more than possible; it is one of the best ways to effect social and systemic change. Relationship-driven and intuitive, it draws on many principles from biomimicry—which you'll hear more about from Austen

White—and emergent leadership. Most importantly, it is founded on a legacy of love, as detailed by Katy Sheehan. If that sounds pie-in-the-sky, or hokey, or trite, remember that love is complex. Love is a labor—one that money can't buy. And it is human to the core. On this subject, seek out chapters by Mary Alberts and Jim himself.

This book also examines the rewards—and hardships—of stewarding a transformational vision. Megan White, Breean Beggs, and Mary Alberts all bluntly examine what happens when innovation is prioritized over best practices. Always choosing the road less traveled can lead to interpersonal and organizational growing pains and be expensive, especially if course correction is time intensive. Also, several projects explored here benefited from 100% start-up funding from developer capital, which made aspects of the mission—like sustainable infrastructure upgrades—easier to achieve, and other aspects—like community buy-in—much harder. On the other hand, these three—along with Austen White, Dave Sanders, and Mariah McKay—praise outcomes too rarely part of the traditional success stories: personal growth, systemic equity, and reduction of harm, to name a few.

This collection of stories is especially poignant in light of the $60 trillion that will be passed on from the Baby Boomers to the next generation in the coming years, as mentioned by John Bjorkman. Like any transition, this change unlocks the possibility of a cultural shift. How do we take advantage of this opportunity? How do we harness the largest transfer of wealth in human history for good? How can we make it easier for members of the 1% to invest in equitable systems at the expense of their personal wealth and power? Part of the solution lies in presenting detailed, on-the-ground examples of experimental and non-traditional philanthropy and community-centered development, which the following chapters set out to do.

The list of contributors to this collection is not comprehensive. Hundreds of people have invested time, insights, and other talents to the CBC, and it feels dishonorable not to mention them all. But to keep the book to a reasonable size, I have excerpted stories from the lives of individuals that are representative of the kind of work that happens on the Community Building Campus. Most chapters were composed through a highly collaborative approach. I conducted a series of interviews and pulled together an initial draft based on those interviews. Then we exchanged drafts until arriving at the final version published here. Rebecca Mack, Kai Huschke, Joe Sheehan, and Katy Sheehan composed their own first drafts, and we edited their chapters together. The book can be read from cover to cover, or readers can skip around to different chapters based on their interests.

However these stories find you, we hope they can demonstrate a more inclusive, more emergent approach to community-driven change. Community Building, after all, is a noun and a verb. It is the place where the community gathers, and it is the people who show up every day to animate and create the space. What follows is a modest excerpt from that chorus of voices. Consider this your invitation to launch your own community campus—or, if you are local to Spokane—to join the latest iteration of the CBC, a story that is yet unfinished and evolving, with unwritten chapters—and contributors—to come.

Part One

Community Building Is a Noun

CHAPTER ONE

The Antidote Is Community

By Jim Sheehan

Jim is the founder of the Community Building Campus and the Center for Justice. He still lives in Spokane and walks to campus most days for coffee and conversation.

If you trace the story of a person's wealth, you will rarely encounter a saint or a hero. In my case, for example, you have to explore the circuitous path of luck and accidents, love and war, Buddhists and civil rights heroes, and a criminal conviction. That story starts with my uncles, James and George, and a special dispensation from the Pope.

In 1907, when he was sixteen years old, my uncle, James Casey, organized friends to work as bicycle couriers so that he could earn extra money to support his family after his father died. As fate would have it, his timing could not have been better. Seattle's population had more than doubled since the turn of the century thanks to the gold rush and railroad. In true capitalist fashion, Casey's company succeeded by undercutting the competition, offering the lowest courier prices in town, and operating twenty-four hours a day, seven days a week, including holidays. By 1912, his company had one hundred employees, and by 1913, its largest client was the United States Postal Service, which had not yet established its own parcel post system. In 1919, Casey opened a branch in Oakland, California, and in 1930, he started servicing the East Coast. By the

1950s, his company—now known as United Parcel Service (UPS)—was the first direct national competitor to the United States Postal Service.

CEOs in America love telling this kind of pick-yourself-up-by-your-bootstraps story, which makes wealth feel inevitable, like Casey was destined for greatness, and that the world needed his vision. But James was not the only Casey, and my money did not come from James Casey directly, or deliberately. His younger brother, George—the less-renowned middle child of the family—married my aunt, Verle Sheehan. She and George were first cousins on his mother's side. The forbidden proximity of their family lineage meant that, in order to get married in the Catholic Church, they had to apply for a special dispensation from the Pope. The Vatican gave its blessing, partly because when Verle was a young woman her pelvis was crushed between two automobiles thanks to a parking brake failure, and she was unable to have children. They married, and Verle joined George in Los Angeles, where he served as President of UPS West Coast, while James moved to New York to run the company out of its new headquarters.

I have few memories of George since he died when I was eleven, but I remember Aunt Verle as a generous, gregarious, but mostly distant relative. When I was a child, I saw her and Uncle George around Thanksgiving each year, when the family gathered at Marguerite Casey's house. (Marguerite was George and James's sister.) I was instructed to be on my best behavior, which meant sit still and keep a sock in it. But the Caseys were all kind to me. Aunt Marguerite asked us questions about our interests and our lives. James, or Uncle Jim to me, always appeared in a three-piece suit, an old regal man sitting comfortably in a wingback chair. As a kid, I always thought it was cool to hang out once a year with the rich people, even if it meant wearing my Sunday best—a crisp white shirt and nice slacks—rather than baseball pants. I think my working-class parents also enjoyed sipping high-end alcohol from polished crystal.

Eventually, I lost touch with Verle after I graduated from Santa Clara. I was drafted to serve in the Vietnam War, then went to law school on the GI Bill, got married, and had a family of my own in Spokane, Washington. I didn't make it a priority to stay in touch and I only saw Verle a few more times before she died in 1997. I learned of her death from my sister, Lolly, who called with the news: of the stock Verle had inherited from her husband and UPS co-founder, George Casey, Verle had bequeathed 5% to me, 5% to my sister, and 5% each to my cousins. She left the rest of that stock to an orphanage in Santa Barbara—the kind of important, but safe, philanthropy I knew I could never commit to.

I sat on the news for a full year before making any financial decisions, digesting the change extensively with my partner at the time, Nancy Schaub, whose family had also left her with some wealth. She was a guide and a teacher in those early days and helped me process the new facts of my life. I also spent a lot of time reflecting on the moments that had delivered me to this exact occasion. I saw wealth as a prism through which I could express my deepest values, but I knew I was going to have to proceed thoughtfully and intuitively if I was going to heed those values and not get distracted by the sudden, nearly limitless possibilities that swirled around me.

When a lot of people start my story here, with the inheritance, I have to rewind to what shaped me, because I know the most important thing about me is not my wealth: it is how I came to learn how to sit, how to be in the present moment, and how to seek wisdom—a wisdom that I started to earn during the war.

*

Despite many peers who protested the conflict, I thought positively about the Vietnam War when my name was drawn and I had to report to the local draft board in 1966. I did not try to seek an exception. But during basic training in New Jersey, it seemed like there weren't any rich kids reporting for duty. Only two of us in the whole platoon were college graduates. After basic training, I started in Officer Candidate School in Maryland, thanks to my college degree and privilege. On weekends I visited a friend who worked as a professor at a women's college in Philadelphia, and during this time I started learning more about current events. Martin Luther King Jr. was at the height of his charisma and power, and I witnessed and even marched in a few civil protests in D.C. at the time. I was waking up.

My values were coalescing around MLK's controversial movement in the 1960s—not the watered-down version of him that many white people elevate today. Everyone knows the quote, "Injustice anywhere is a threat to justice everywhere," but the rest of the quote shows how revolutionary King really was: "We are caught in an inescapable network of mutuality, tied in a single garment of destiny. Whatever affects one directly, affects all indirectly." He called out society's attempts to separate us, and tried to envision a world where we no longer organized ourselves around toxic ideas that aggravate this separation. The MLK I knew was radical, countercultural, and one of my biggest heroes. I believe that his greatest contribution was and is as a mystic. In one way or another, he always dwelled on the themes of oneness, connection, and community. The deeper truths of his call to unity started to sink in then, and are a major driver in my life now.

In the midst of the struggle for civil rights, our nation was also deeply divided by the war I was fighting. Everyone had an opinion, but some people in power were benefiting financially from the military industrial complex while others suffered or lost their lives. As I was on the path to becoming a detachment commander at Fort Bragg, it seemed everyone I encountered was either going to Vietnam, waiting to go, or returning. I requested to go to Fort Bragg because I wanted to jump out of airplanes. As a young man, I thought that would be really cool, but I flunked the physical because I had sliding joints. It should have disqualified me, but the military transferred me to a unit supporting the 82nd Airborne. I got fully trained and was ready to deploy, but for some reason I never got the orders to ship out to Vietnam. I graduated top of my class at Officer Candidate School, and should have been the first one taken, but I never went. That bizarre stroke of luck was one of several key moments when things could have gone very differently for me.

My biggest change in consciousness came from this time, from staying in the U.S., watching the careless assignment of human bodies, and bearing witness to who was really fighting our war. I listened to what was said by politicians but saw what was really happening. While boys like me stayed home, the number of minority soldiers sent to Vietnam was completely skewed. So many of them were Black, and decades later we now know that Black soldiers were more likely to be sent to the front lines, more likely to be disciplined, and less likely to be promoted. The disparity was dramatic, and it profoundly affected my worldview.

I did a one-eighty in the military. I was lucky in that I was always curious, always researched, always wondered, and was always interested in truth. But the military was a shock; it was so drastically different from everything I had been taught about it. They break you down and re-create you. You start as a smart, creative, intelligent person, and you become a non-questioning, compliant entity so that you don't tune into the moral traumas or dwell on the sanctity of life. But once I was out, back in society as a civilian again, I bore witness to these traumas, to the number of guys being sent overseas and to far fewer returning. I did not experience war firsthand with them, but I paid attention to them, absorbed their losses, and at my best have been empathetic and have not looked away. Not looking away is a muscle, a skill that must be practiced, and it has served me my whole life.

Courtesy of Hamilton Studios

The Community Building's founder, Jim Sheehan

*

After a year of meditation and counsel following my inheritance, I intuited that the best way to start approximating truth in my decision-making and actions would be to do what I know. I decided to open a nonprofit law firm. If I was a plumber, I would have opened a nonprofit plumbing firm. But law firms weren't perfect models for the way I wanted to be present to people and their stories. I had to draw on my experience with Eddie, and dozens of other men and women like him, for guidance.

I was assigned to Eddie's case in 1985 while working as a public defender for the City of Spokane. Eddie was accused of kidnapping a six-year-old girl from her bedroom, murdering her, then abandoning her body in a nearby dump. The horror of this scene, and the ensuing demand for justice, swept across the city like a wildfire on a windy day in August. Unabating media coverage piled on more fuel, and Eddie, by way of public opinion, was guilty before the trial even started. My job was to blow away as much smoke as possible so the jury could fairly engage the facts of the case and see my client more clearly.

Many people have asked me over the years how I could defend hardened criminals. This question exposes a conflict in how we conceive of and practice justice. Imagine living in a society where defendants don't get representation or rights to a trial. Imagine a world where the police, judges, and jury could convict people without a full examination of evidence. In my twenty-two-year legal career, I came to realize that the protection of human rights was extremely important, and that those rights were protected by the defense, not the prosecution. We had to put constraints on the government, or those in power could do whatever they wanted, imprison whomever they wanted, and pardon whomever they wanted. My job was to uphold the cornerstone of the justice system in America—an America where every woman receives equal protection under the law, where every man is innocent until proven guilty.

In Eddie's case, though, I wasn't trying to preserve the constitutional rights of a man who had probably done it but still deserved due process; I was trying to keep an innocent man from going to prison. I knew for a fact that Eddie didn't do it, and I had a pretty good idea of who did. But people's deeply held fears, which darkened to plumes of anger, were overwhelming. The jury quickly convicted Eddie and sentenced him to life in prison. We appealed the case and geared up for another trial in 1990, where he was found guilty again.

I could have walked away from the case. I had done my due diligence of trying to free Eddie, but I couldn't let it rest. It wasn't Eddie's fault that the system had failed, and that as a result a large amount of city resources were tied up in his case. So, in 1994, nine years after Eddie's first trial, we prepared for a third. This time, I was sure Eddie would be exonerated.

The primary witness in the first and second trial was the girl's brother, who was four years old at the time of the crime. Given his age and the influence of the adults in his life, he was an unreliable witness. Now fourteen years old, the brother was able to think for himself, and he admitted that his mother and the lead detective had influenced his testimony. After removing the brother's testimony, all the remaining evidence was circumstantial and radically inconsistent. The only things holding the case together were the egos of law enforcement and the prosecution, who did not want to have on their consciences sentencing an innocent man to life in prison.

Situations like this, in the theater of the courtroom, remind me of the attorneys who have influenced me. Images of the Maycomb, Alabama courtroom come to mind, along with Atticus Finch's closing argument: "I have nothing but pity in my heart for the chief witness for the state, but my pity does not extend so far as to her putting a man's life at stake, which she has done in an effort to get rid of her own guilt." In the case of my client, the guilt was different—the woman accusing my client was acting out of the loss of her daughter. But much like the injustice in *To Kill a Mockingbird*, someone had to pay. Eddie, a soft-spoken vagrant with a record of non-violent crimes, was a disposable character in the eyes of society and the easiest person to blame.

Fortunately, Eddie, unlike the fictional Tom Robinson, was not executed in the end. However, his tenure in prison was replete with suffering. He had been locked away in isolation in the Washington State Penitentiary for nine years since men who are found guilty of crimes like the one Eddie was convicted of are beaten and sometimes murdered in a general population. And his story is still tragic in my eyes since Eddie was never exonerated. The prosecution put together a plea deal that gave him credit for time served and the chance to walk out of prison within a few days, and he took it.

When Eddie took the plea deal, I was devastated on his behalf, but I understood. He never should have been in prison in the first place, and this was the quickest way out. Had he opted to see the sentence reversed, Eddie would have had to go back to jail for two to three months while we staged the trial, with no way to 100% guarantee that he would be acquitted.

Although Eddie's case was dramatic, I was involved with many others like it in my career as a public defender, first in Everett, and then in Spokane. Cases like Eddie's helped me see that the law isn't actually that concerned with justice. Justice happens sometimes—certainly more than sometimes—but the primary value of law is order. This is a scary concept because the dominant culture decides what defines order. The prosecution used the dominant culture in Spokane—a culture where we pretend bad things don't happen, and someone must pay as quickly as possible when they do—to convict Eddie.

Over the years, I saw a strong connection between justice and community. If we are going to provide experiences of justice, we have to understand that people who make poor choices are in need of connection. Instead, our criminal justice system further segregates even non-violent offenders. Injustice is really separation—separation from truth, from dignity, from the true self, and from community. If we are going to give people the chance to truly recover, heal, and reform, we cannot only judge their actions and separate them from ourselves. The human way to address crime is through restoration and recognizing that we are all One. We have to transcend rational concepts and be present to our One-ness.

*

The ultimate guide for me through this journey into wealth is my sitting and meditation practice. Some expressions of Buddhism say you move incrementally

Jim Sheehan with Van Jones at a Center for Justice fundraiser

Photo by Robert Zeller

toward enlightenment; others say it's instantaneous, a gift that can happen at any time. I believe that enlightenment is always present, but we're not always aware of it. Enlightenment is who we are.

I'm thankful for my early encounters with Catholic mystics because they expanded my spirituality. Great mystical writers in Catholic teachings speak to experiences of enlightenment. I had been raised Catholic, and the prayerful aphorisms of Eckhart and the like were an invitation, a way of exploring spirituality without boundaries, a way to experience truth without the weight of dogma and the limitations of ego and self. What I have always wanted is to go deep, to reach down with courage and honesty, and to be present to what is there. To go into that silence, to the place where there can be no difference between people.

One of the greatest challenges of my life is distilling the experience of One-ness into action, into how I express love toward others and direct the resources at my disposal. Like Thomas Merton—though not as poetically as he—I struggle with how to engage the world around me while honoring the "wisdom of emptiness." I experience truth while sitting and meditating, but like most people in the world, I also have to get up.

Through the Center for Justice, I was able to fulfill a long-held desire to do more for my town and its most vulnerable citizens, to do more for those whose experiences with law trended more towards order than towards justice. But I have always known that the law is only one vehicle for achieving Justice—an imperfect, expensive vehicle—and that I wanted to take a much more holistic approach to effecting social change.

So, I sat again. I thought some more. And I knew that I needed a building.

There weren't any beautiful, affordable offices for nonprofits in Spokane's downtown core, and certainly not places set aside with an inclusive community in mind. In 1998, I bought an old building on Main Avenue, restored it, named it "Community Building," settled my nonprofit as the anchor tenant on the third floor, and invited several other nonprofits to join us.

Creating inclusive spaces has been a way to translate truth and justice into action. The moment, the present, the now does have a place. The place becomes all important because it is part of One-ness, wherever it is experienced. If love and compassion are the genuine motives for our activities, then hopefully we are channeling—however imperfectly, as much as we are able—our One-ness into brick and mortar.

Today's Community Building Campus is to me what Cornel West meant when he said, "Justice is what love looks like in public." This book is a celebration of Community Building, a look at what can happen when personal wealth is leveraged as a community resource. For the last twenty years, we have hosted, inspired, and catalyzed local change. The chapters in this book explore the countercultural and evolving nature of this two-decade experiment, of which I have been a small but continuous part.

My hope is that the next generation of change agents will be inspired by our imperfect but genuine pursuit of this underlying concept: that the antidote to the cultural ills of our society is community, and that the core of community is love.

Recently, I looked back to a journal I wrote in occasionally throughout the '90s and came across an entry dated shortly after I received my inheritance. I was thankful that the strokes of my life had led me to ask the following questions:

What is important?

What can we do, for ourselves and for others?

What is the responsibility?

How should we live?

Without a family that instilled me with love, a career that exposed me to deep suffering, and a meditation practice that helped me engage on a regular basis with the deepest possible truth, mine may have been a very different story. The questions we ask and revisit profoundly affect the unfolding of our lives, and the trajectory of the work we invest in. Thankfully, the questions I asked led me into a more creative and inclusive interpretation of what's possible and what wealth is for.

Our project is just one of many ways to ground money in place to co-create spaces that nurture our communities. It is from this humble stature that I offer the work we've done in Spokane as a living model—a model that has expanded and evolved and will continue to do so, especially as the next generation infuses its wisdom.

CHAPTER TWO

One-Block Revolution

By Rebecca Mack

Rebecca has been a member of the CBC team for the last ten years in a jack-of-all-trades role, helping to nurture and sustain community connections. She also hosted a community affairs talk show on KYRS, led the creation and development of the CBC's first website, and helped address neighborhood safety issues.

Sometimes it's not capitalists and tycoons that manage miraculous revitalization, but a loose confederation of ordinary men and women. In Spokane's case, there were a handful of pioneering types who nursed a new vision for a particularly derelict part of downtown. One by one, without formal organization, they decided to plant their energy and money in the easternmost block of West Main Avenue.

If you rubberneck a little as you stroll the extra wide sidewalks at the eastern fringe of downtown Spokane, there are clues to its roller coaster history. The brick facades of the sturdy old buildings lining Main Avenue are shot with faded billboard ads for flour, cigars, and tobacco, and for single rooms for rent at the Hotel Saranac. The residents of the single-room occupancy hotels (SROs) in the early 1900s were good customers for the dry goods—mainstays of the working-class laborers of the neighborhood who migrated to Spokane to help build the region's emerging industries. Abundant natural resources and the confluence of rivers and rail lines stoked a boom in the Inland Northwest.

Nowadays, there are lots of eager customers back in the neighborhood and a bonanza of shopping choices. Most everything offered back in the olden days is still on offer. Customers are still looking for whole foods and basics, and can find organic, locally grown flour and meat, bottled milk, eggs, coffee, and fresh produce at Spokane's only food co-op. Shoppers can pick up freshly prepared foods for take-out or check out neighborhood tips and events from the community corkboard jammed with notices and notes. It's easy to happen on a friend or neighbor at multiple shared tables or find a quiet corner for a cup of soup.

The story of how a single block evolved over the course of more than a century cannot be easily summarized. While its physical size is small—only the easternmost block of West Main Avenue—its community impact in the last two decades is substantial. Its transformation from a dirty, intimidating jumble of derelict buildings and dark alleys to a vibrant, welcoming community has radiated out a kind of synergistic effect on the rest of Spokane.

The details that follow, although commonplace at times, demonstrate that grassroots, community-led change is incremental and ongoing. All kinds of people over the decades have been attracted to the block—immigrants and homesteaders, businessmen and laborers, merchants and customers, residents and vagrants. The succession of individuals did not necessarily have a grand plan or shared vision. But the particular mix and history of all those people over all those years somehow had the alchemy to bring the block to the serendipitous point in time that it finds itself at today.

A Reporter's Take

As a reporter at Spokane's ABC affiliate with my ear to the ground in the late '90s, I'd heard about a former Spokane public defender who'd inherited a boatload of money and founded a nonprofit law firm. He was also reported to be restoring a dilapidated old brick building on the east side of downtown to house the growing law firm and offer space to other nonprofits.

The building he was working on at 35 West Main had most recently housed a brewery and eatery, and young people who had never ventured downtown sought it out. They seemed to enjoy braving the littered sidewalks in the sketchy neighborhood to sample the beer and bar food served in baskets lined with crinkly red and white checked paper.

I'd been to the Birkenbeiner Brewery myself, so I was curious. What kind of nutjob buys a building that needs a ton of work in a crummy neighborhood? Why didn't this lucky heir take his money and go buy a yacht or something?

Our station had a program back then featuring live radio interviews with local newsmakers. Somehow, we got Jim Sheehan on the phone for a five-minute 'Live at Five' interview. While prepping in the studio, my middle-aged, conservative, white guy, radio veteran cohorts practically snorted their shared derision. Even before we put Jim on the air, they concluded that he had more money than sense and mocked his hippie quest. My co-host was polite enough during the interview but barely concealed his incredulity at Jim's plans for a Center for Justice in Spokane.

Jim unabashedly described his vision for 35 West Main as a place for underrepresented people needing a voice and as a place to create community. As a public defender, he described how he'd witnessed gut-wrenching injustice. The accused were routinely denied a fair shake because they could not afford good legal help. He felt he could best give back to his home community by starting a nonprofit law firm. He said things like, "If anyone in a culture is oppressed, then we're all oppressed." There was a lot of eye rolling in the studio.

If Jim sensed disrespect through the phone line, he didn't show it. He affably answered all questions about his vision for peace, justice, and community building. I was struck by his modesty and sense of humor. I was also amazed that he actually talked about love. The old guys in the newsroom casually dismissed Jim as a passing curiosity, doomed to fail. Oddly enough, I now work with and for him. My time with Jim and the Community Building has afforded me the chance to do some of the most rewarding work of my life. But twenty years ago, back at the studio, I set myself to learning more about my adopted town.

Historical Development

In 1889, downtown Spokane burned to rubble in a great fire. The catastrophe turned out to be a blessing in disguise in some regards, and the fire destroyed substandard buildings and wiped the slate clean. There was money and energy for redevelopment, and the city's captains of industry rebuilt downtown into a sturdy, thriving hub in a matter of just a few years.

In the '20s, Spokane continued to prosper as the hub of the Inland Northwest, the largest city between Minneapolis and Seattle. Fortunes were made in mining, timber, and agriculture. Beautiful homes and commercial buildings were built with top-notch craftsmanship and the finest materials—vertical grain fir, oak, mahogany, basalt, as well as paving and building bricks created and fired locally—some right out of a cavernous pit in a tony South Hill neighborhood.

Old photos show handsome brick buildings and bustling streets with throngs of pedestrians, street cars, small businesses, and shops fronting the main streets of downtown. The influx of capital and jobs brought by the boom days of natural resource development gradually dwindled, and a period of stagnation and slow decline followed. Our city has long struggled to revive its heyday.

Downtown Spokane scored a small boom when it hosted Expo '74, officially known as the International Exposition on the Environment. The months-long event was the first environmentally themed world's fair and attracted roughly 5.6 million people to Spokane. To accommodate a world-class event, the huge tangle of rail yards and accompanying toxic waste was removed. The iconic clock tower in the center of the yards remained, and the rest of the site alongside the Spokane River was restored and replaced with a pavilion, ice rink, parklands, and gleaming modern attractions.

Because of Expo '74, the central downtown core attracted new investors who developed large bank buildings and conventional businesses such as national department store chains and restaurants. But before long, the event seemed to be the last gasp of a bustling downtown, and Spokane residents were lured to outlying areas to live and shop. The "malling of America" enticed residents and shoppers to outlying areas, and downtown slid into a period of high vacancy rates and empty streets. Walking around downtown did not feel safe to many. The few people who ventured there complained about having to pay for parking and preferred the skywalks to the sidewalks.

The skywalks that arched over Main Avenue were meant to allow pedestrians to cross between buildings and insulate them from the weather. Spokane's skywalks were modeled after the successful skywalk system in Minneapolis and helped draw people to shop downtown. At one point, the system was the second largest in the United States. It turned out that the highly touted skywalks had the unintended consequence of further harming downtown vitality. They plucked pedestrians from the street, which wiped out the energy and security that comes from a bustling sidewalk environment. People went from their homes to parking garages to the skywalks and lost their connection to the guts of the city.

Photo by Rajah Bose

The handsome brick facade of the old Hotel Saranac building

Eventually, though, the skywalks lost their allure, and the small businesses that once occupied them closed up shop. By the mid-1990s, Spokane residents had pretty much lost interest in downtown—its streets, skywalks, and sidewalks.

Consequently, many historic downtown buildings went dark, fell into disrepair, and were razed. For example, the Rookery and adjoining Mohawk Building were destroyed in 2004, in spite of ardent efforts by preservationists. The Mohawk (1915) was a seven-story, steel-frame structure, a prime example of the Chicago School style of architecture. According to the Spokane Historic Preservation Office, the Rookery (1934) was "the premier Spokane example of terra cotta artistry employing Art Deco design elements." Designed by Gustav Pehrson, it was a rare example of high-style design in a downtown commercial building. On Riverside Avenue at Howard, in the heart of downtown, the Mohawk and Rookery were demolished by owner Wendell Reugh, who claimed to have plans to rebuild. Steve Gill, property manager for Reugh at the time, said in a *Spokesman-Review* story that the property would be best as a multi-use development, and potential investors were waiting for demolition. Historic preservation, he said, just wasn't "financially feasible." Today, the vacant sites are occupied by surface parking lots.

The loss of the Mohawk and the Rookery to the wrecking ball motivated

Spokane City Council. They adopted an ordinance restricting demolition of downtown historic buildings, and the tide began to turn back in favor of downtown and its historic idiosyncrasies. The erstwhile outliers on the east end of West Main were de facto leaders in this wave of renewed appreciation.

Development Today

Just like in the old days, the east block of West Main still has several drinking establishments of all types, specializing in everything from craft beer brewed on-site to fine whiskey. At last count, there are at least three places to get coffee, three bakeries, five restaurants, an ice cream shop, and a sandwich shop. There are multiple retail establishments, including a plant and flower shop, native arts emporium, thrift store, comics and games store, fair trade store, lighting store, and a dress and jewelry boutique. There's a yoga studio, acupuncturist, palm reader, art gallery, beauty salons, child care center, and an independent movie theater. There are residential apartments on the upper floors of three of the oldest buildings on the block. More than forty nonprofits enjoy beautiful, unique office spaces, shared kitchens, meeting rooms, and outdoor dining and event spots on the upper floors of the Saranac and Community Buildings.

It's important to acknowledge that this is not the work of just one person. Several unconventional entrepreneurs risked locating in the sketchy neighborhood outside the central business district. It took guts and vision to pioneer new investment there, and each person who took the leap helped to fortify the overall commitment. A kind of synergy naturally developed that continues to this day.

Dan Spalding was among the first in this transformational wave when he bought the Longbotham Building at 22 West Main. Spalding grew up in Spokane into a family that owned the largest auto wrecking yard in Eastern Washington. He variously describes himself as an artist, musician, and real estate developer. Constructed in 1909, the Longbotham (then known as the Frederick Hotel) was designed with tradesmen in mind. The single-room occupancy building provided fifty-seven residential rooms on the upper floors and provided street-level rental spaces to local businesses. For decades it was one of the most successful and prominent Japanese-owned businesses in Spokane.

James Gutner, another early joiner, took a chance in 1993 when he opened his microbrewery at 35 West Main. Six years later, Jim Sheehan bought 35

West Main, which he renamed the Community Building. Revival Lighting partners—Janine Vaughn, John Hahn, and David Farmer—bought the 14 West Main building in 2002, after a three-year stint around the corner on Division, at the Belle Franklin. Janine says the former machine shop, seat cover maker, and antique store attracted them because "there was basically nothing in this end of town, and it was affordable."

John Waite bought 19 West Main in 2003 and opened Merlyn's, his quirky comic book store. He then bought 7 West Main in 2010, took up residence on the second floor, and started renovations on the rest of his building, including some apartments on the second floor. John is an entrepreneur, for sure, but he is first and foremost a community builder.

"What defines me," John says, "is hard work, being honest, helping others. I am also into efficiency and systems running properly and allocating resources so they're the most beneficial to everybody, not just to me or a segment of the population."

In 2004, Jim Sheehan bought the Hotel Saranac at 25 West Main, which was built in or around 1909 by Coulee City businessman Hiram H. Hutton to meet the demand for cheap housing and was home to individuals from all over the world. While the upper floors housed visitors and residents, the lower floor was leased out to Japanese- and Chinese-owned businesses, including the City Hand Laundry and the North Coast Supply Company. A few years after Harry Hutton's death, the Saranac building was sold in 1947 to Norboru Hayashi, one of several bought by Japanese-American families after World War II.

The once dilapidated, single-room occupancy, residential hotel is now a thriving eco-friendly community building. When restoration was completed in 2006, the Saranac became the first LEED Platinum-certified building in the Inland Northwest. In a characteristic twist, multiple five-panel doors from the old Hotel Saranac that could not be used in its restoration were offered to Dan Spalding across the street at the Longbotham. In his usual inventive style, Spalding repurposed them into tabletops at Boots Bakery & Lounge.

Also in 2006, Jim Sheehan bought the Goodyear Tire Store across the street at Main and Browne. The old tire store is now the Main Market Co-op, Spokane's only co-op grocery store. Main Market focuses on fresh, locally sourced products, an organic salad bar, and ready-to-eat offerings from its bustling on-site kitchen. Keeping with Sheehan's commitment to incorporating sustainability and beauty into design, the Main Market features solar panels, a greenhouse on its roof, and a vibrant mural on its west side.

Rebecca Mack, the CBC's jack of all trades

Sheehan bought his next building, 17 West Main, in 2007. He later swapped it with John Waite for 19 West Main, a move that added further momentum to the neighborhood. The swap consolidated each property owner's buildings into contiguous stretches. Both built on the spirit of what was already taking place—a spirit of neighborliness and local connection.

19 West Main, now known as the Saranac Commons, opened in 2015. Centered on the block, its large front doors, skylights, and open interior harken to its beginnings as an auto repair shop. It has become something of a gathering place, featuring a funky common space with exposed brick, fireplace, and open-beamed ceilings. The centerpiece of the space is made from 1,500 antique bottles that Brian Martin extracted from the banks of the Spokane River. During the last days of his life, Valerie Wahl from the Northwest Museum of Arts and Culture helped Brian curate his collection. Local blacksmith-artist Alex Robinson then suspended the bottles with hand-forged copper and steel and grouped them into a hanging chandelier that catches the sun's rays through layers of multicolored glass.

The block has slowly taken shape as an outpost of small, independent enterprises housed in old buildings that were restored but not "remuddled." While there was no explicit agreement about how the block would fashion itself, it has serendipitously evolved to feature a unique identity. Important to its sustainability is that the people who have invested in the neighborhood live and work there still and are caring and active in its day to day. They bump into each other on the sidewalk and rub elbows at the pub.

Attracting a New Wave of City Investment

Many attempts have been made to come up with an edgy moniker for this section of town. But the block's unique identity has defied attempts to brand it in a way that would lend itself to banners and brochures. As cities around the country are racing to brand downtown districts, and the block's popularity has grown, the City of Spokane has at various times hired consultants to come up with a brand name and slogan for the district, but nothing has stuck. It is still referred to in various ways: East/West Main, East End, Groovy Town, etc. As if in concert with the block's outlier status, its unique character has defied neat categorization.

These neighbors on West Main tend not to be "joiners" or organizers of traditional business groups. Their independent natures, which brought them to the block in the first place, persist. However, there are a few guiding principles that most everyone on the block shares. Janine Vaughn of Revival sums it up pretty well: "Everybody here cares about inviting people to come into the neighborhood and feel welcome and relaxed. We care about community and the environment. We value aesthetics and take care of our places. It's a progressive neighborhood, and we love that."

These shared values were key to uniting residents, tenants, and business and property owners behind a city project that radically changed the configuration of West Main. Neighbors John Waite, Jim Sheehan, Dan Spalding, and CBC community coordinator Dave Sanders (Chapter 5) had for decades envisioned restoring their block between Browne and Division to its historic configuration as a two-way street, or even possibly turning it over to people altogether and making it a pedestrian mall. But even as the block began to flourish, the four-lane, one-way thoroughfare of West Main that runs on the east end remained bleakly unchanged as a featureless arterial.

That is, until Councilman Jon Snyder put his shoulder to the wheel at city hall on our behalf in 2015. He maintained that there were areas of downtown outside the conventional core that were deserving of more attention and investment focus. Jon was a long-time champion of the Community Building and focused his advocacy on the east end of West Main. He was the founding chair of KYRS Thin Air Community Radio (Chapter 9) and his kids attended the Community Building Children's Center (Chapter 8).

The Saranac Building lobby during construction and after completion

"The property owners on that block were really invested in the success of the entire block," says Snyder. "They weren't absentee landlords. Dan and John live there, and Jim might as well live there for all the time he spends down there," he adds, chuckling. "As an elected official, the most important commodity I had was time. I wanted to invest my time where I thought we had the greatest chance of success, and that was the project on the east end of West Main."

Councilman Snyder ardently advocated for the city to recognize the amount of private investment on West Main and knew firsthand that a small, loosely affiliated group of local businesspeople were dedicated to their block. He believed the city should express recognition and appreciation by allocating public time, talent, and treasure to the block. Councilman Snyder helped secure $60,000 in parking meter money for streetscape improvement and recruited people in the neighborhood to lend support.

The Ongoing Work of Community-Centered Development

In January 2015, I met with Councilman Snyder, Merlyn's owner John Waite, and City Planner Inge Note at Boots Bakery to hatch a plan for change on our block. Jim Sheehan's role was to commit the resources, which basically amounted to staff time (me) to organize and guide the neighborhood to articulate and unite behind a shared vision for the block. Note's primary goal was to make Spokane more bike-friendly. We hunched around a small table and mulled over the options. We started out with the idea of adding a bike lane to our block and possibly reconfiguring parking.

Multiple meetings followed, and a vast array of configurations were considered by a changing cast of characters. These meetings involved people commonly called stakeholders in modern parlance: neighbors, business owners, city staffers, residents, tenants, property owners, bike advocates, art patrons, and political types. All and sundry came and went from these meetings over the course of the next several months. Lots of sketching, brainstorming, and walking the neighborhood was involved.

Crucially, Councilman Snyder was committed to consistently push for the project politically as long as he could count on neighborhood support. Just as crucially, there was a small core group that showed up at every meeting and stayed involved with every aspect of the project from beginning to end. This consistency of commitment was critical, as was our pragmatism in dealing with the excruciatingly slow and laborious process of navigating all the hoops of bureaucracy in a historically conservative city.

In August 2015, the city stepped up its financial contribution to the improvement project and allocated an additional $120,000 to the $60,000 of parking meter money. As the design and scope of the project evolved, it changed significantly, and this made some people unhappy. The dedicated bike lane was modified to a "sharrow," a lane shared by autos and bikes—not the preference of bike advocates. The proposed mid-block crossing was untried in Spokane and problematic for landscaping and signage, which upset public safety officials. The middle-of-the-block angled parking was also brand new to Spokane, and city engineers refused to stamp the design for it, citing safety and snow-removal issues. Business owners were upset about the potential impact of street construction on parking and access. City officials began to call it a "Pilot Project," our understanding being that the project was so radical, city officials wanted people to understand that the whole thing could be "scraped" if it was later deemed to be a failure. (The city warned they could bring in a machine that would literally scrape all elements of the project away so the street would regain its "flat as a pancake" profile.)

The city began to balk at the apparent lack of unity and support. At more than one point that autumn, it looked as though the whole project might fall apart. Our little core group decided we had to take the lead in creating unity and convened what we called a Summit Meeting to gain support for a shared mission statement for the block.

We planned our meeting carefully. We made personal contact with supporters and detractors. In other words, we counted our votes. In surprisingly short order, we were able to get agreement from everyone that no matter what differences we might have in our specific notions of what should and should not be included in our block design, we all shared a common goal: to make our little neighborhood less a vehicle thoroughfare and more a safe and friendly oasis for walkers, bikers, businesspeople, and plants. The meeting was attended by an impressive number of diverse interests that eventually voted to "support traffic-calming streetscape enhancements that improve parking access and pedestrian and bicycle safety on our block."

The folks at City Hall eventually decided that investing in our block was a good risk. Two years of meetings, advocacy, and disruptive construction activity resulted in the completion of a project that turned the four-lane, one-way stretch of Main between Browne and Division into a dramatically different experience for walkers, bikers, and motorists. The project was hard on businesses because the street had to be closed for a time, but it was worth it in the long run. The unity of business and property owners and the tenants helped the city maintain its political will to transform the block's traffic and parking configuration. In addition to our stated iron will about our shared mission, we also demonstrated our flexibility in considering options, and our ability to compromise.

*

Sometimes when I run into Jim Sheehan around the Community Building Campus, having coffee at the Commons, or a bite to eat at the Main Market, I think about that day twenty years ago when we had him on the radio, and he talked about his vision for a fringe block on West Main. I think about my co-host who said something like, "A fool and his money are soon parted." And while Jim may have parted with money to bring his vision to life, his gift to our entire Spokane community is an investment that keeps on giving. As the block evolves, it's clear that it's not the product of a strategic real estate development designed to make money for investors. Rather, it is people working together to create community.

CHAPTER THREE

Beauty and Inclusion in People-Centered Spaces

By Patsy O'Connor

Patsy is the architect who worked side-by-side with Jim on every project in the six-building campus and also on his personal home design and build. She now serves as an architect and consultant on other shared-space projects like the Carl Maxey Center.

I am an architect by training, and I love rehabbing buildings. In my work with clients, I enjoy figuring out what they need, how they need to be in or use the new space, and how we can best accommodate the intersection of desires and values. My ethic is: I don't design for me; I design for you. The project is for the client. Discussion is the first step, and a huge part of my design process. You have to find a commonality of words, vision, and visuals to help make a language that both designer and client can understand and get behind.

Jim is an unusual collaborator because he does not provide specific stipulations for most aspects of his vision. Instead, he describes a feeling. He doesn't talk about what he wants or how he thinks you should get there. He talks in a kind of spiritual circle. He'll say, "I want it to feel like this; I want people to want to come to the buildings; I want everyone to feel comfortable." It's my job to spend enough time talking with him and being in the space to figure out what that means on a practical level. For every Community Building project, there has been a common thread, and for Jim that was: *make it beautiful and desirable to the community.* Sometimes he wouldn't get much more specific than that.

Fortunately, Jim is willing to commit to a budget that supports the whole process, from design to opening the doors. A lot of developers are much more tuned into the bottom line and turning as much profit as possible, which means they aren't as invested in the non-financial outcomes of the project. They might be interested in using recycled or sustainable materials, but if the budget gets tight, sustainability is often the first thing to go. At the end of the day, they're thinking about how they can get a building up with the least amount of money involved.

I think people finally see the consequences of developing with only the bottom line in mind, and things are starting to change. Sustainability is a big part of making things from the heart, and energy from the heart is better than energy from the pocketbook.

Comfort and Inclusivity

When I worked for Jim, he was the client because he was financing the projects, but the buildings weren't for him. We designed everything with the community in mind. To do this, you have to understand the existing building, the neighborhood vibe, and the people you are designing the building for. You also have to accept that the project might evolve and change over time. This is hard for a lot of developers to conceive of, let alone design for, but it's an important part of creating buildings that aren't for you. Usually, you can create a lot of that feeling with color, and with the size and balance of interior spaces.

For example, you'll notice a lot of red and green when you walk into the buildings. Red and green are not direct opposites on the color wheel, but they're very complementary to each other. So long as you select the right tone, red and green work well together because we experience complementary colors as soothing. We keep carrying that color scheme into each new building because those reds and greens do what we need them to do. They're calming and reassuring, and they're not overstepping their bounds by trying to draw attention or absorb all the impact themselves; they're a nice, mellow background for what's going on around them. They allow people and activities to take center stage.

One of the upfront requests for the Community Building was to make it feel comfortable, and to make it feel comfortable for all people. Jim wanted to

Architect and consultant, Patsy O'Connor

appeal to a broad scope of people at different stages in their lives—including clients of nonprofit organizations seeking assistance who might be tired, sick, or part of that whole myriad of situations that make people feel or act defensive. Keeping that in mind, we wanted to evoke a homey, warm feeling—nothing cold or institutional. Jim described the range of cases they might come across at the Center for Justice, which was the Community Building's anchor tenant. A lot of the Center's clients were people in crisis, and we wanted to actively soothe them before they even arrived at the office. The building already had a lot of warm wood tones that we worked with, and Jim wanted to use earth tones throughout. We used a medium density for the colors, which had a quieting effect.

Balance is another aspect of design that impacts how people feel in a space. Balance is the distribution of visual impact, through color or the use of objects, which can make a space feel stable. Some people strive to achieve this in a very formal way through symmetry. Another approach is to give both sides of a space some kind of visual weight, though not through exact copying.

Part of getting to know what makes a space feel right and good to other people is to understand their need for balance. I've known some people who had to have everything symmetrical. They say things like, "There's a window here, so there has to be a window this many inches off-center on the other side." It has to be that way. But you can achieve balance in other ways. For example, if you have a room that's uniformly pink but you want to accentuate one part of the room, you can add lighting on one side. You've thrown it out of balance, in a way. But if you add a seating area to one side—let's say you have artwork on one side with bright light; and on the other side, a seating area with low light—it will feel balanced because of the strength of each of the components. The strength of the light on one side and furniture mass on the other also achieves balance. At the Community Building, we aimed to make spaces feel balanced and inviting.

Jim was so obsessed with people feeling comfortable that he even wanted to extend this to the bathrooms. I couldn't do plain tile everywhere since I knew that would not achieve the effect he was after, so I came up with this idea: instead of just focusing on the walls, we'd treat the floor like home. We installed sections of mosaic tile like a rug in front of your sink at home. It mimics that warm home feel without putting rugs in every bathroom of a commercial facility. To make things more interesting, Jim asked me to incorporate tiles made by a friend of his, along with some reclaimed, recycled tiles. This restriction gave me a different box of tools to work with and generated a unique outcome.

Since the Community Building was interdisciplinary in nature from the beginning, we were able to approach the entire project as multi-use, and we kept flexibility at the front of our minds. Flexibility is a difficult concept to define and to accept, let alone design for. But it's an important concept when you're creating buildings for an evolving community. In the case of the Community Building and Saranac Buildings, flexibility meant designing for the original tenants—who gave us someone to design for and helped keep the space stable as other organizations transitioned into the building—but also accepting that the project would evolve and change, like the ebb and flow of organizations across time.

Defensible Space: A Holistic Approach

Another aspect of designing for comfort and inclusivity is considering defensible space. People often feel more comfortable in a smaller space than a larger one. A lot of people like to go into a place and sit in the corner where they can see the comings and goings. People watching, and having awareness of our surroundings, can give us a sense of comfort. So there are a lot of dynamics related to psychology and human behavior that are important to keep in mind, as well.

When Jim and I started working together, the "defensible space" approach was popular. Scholars theorized about why some people who live in tenements in certain areas of big cities sometimes vandalize or neglect them, and why outdoor common spaces are sometimes appropriated for unwanted or illicit behaviors. Out of those studies came a theory of design that encourages people to enter and exit the space quickly, rather than lingering or hanging out. And it's all about color, lighting, surface materials, and textures. I find it fascinating—especially how broadly the approach can be applied. For example, when restaurants want a fast customer overturn, they use certain colors. If they want them to hang out, they use different colors.

I had the defensible space theory in mind, but we flipped it on its head. Our goal was to also use architecture to encourage certain behaviors. But rather than crime prevention—an absence of behaviors—we wanted to inspire people to build relationships. We wanted to actively encourage and inspire the community through the built environment.

I knew that when parts of buildings are not watched or used regularly, then this leftover space can fall into decay or promote isolation. I tried to make sure there were no unwatched spaces, and I used the defensible space theory in combination with what I knew about Jim. The tricky part was making sure that it all still felt beautiful. But it's hard to really say what's beautiful and what's not. Beauty is subjective, so I tried to find this balance of symmetrical and asymmetrical, defensible and indefensible, beautiful and useful.

In the Community Building, this approach was successful. The lobby windows are huge so you can see in, making it feel open and welcoming. Inside, you find multiple, varied seating spaces—one that has a kitchen table feel, and another arranged like comfy couches around a fireplace, which makes for an interesting entry. In contrast, many office buildings enter into a nondescript hallway or elevators. At the Community Building, you have a space that's undefined, which invites curiosity and makes visitors want to linger. It's welcoming without saying so. You walk by and want to poke your head in. My eyes are drawn to the mezzanine and balcony, which draw people farther into the building. Children are often in the space, and the Kizuri (Chapter 11) staff also open their doors to the lobby with a bright display of colorful clothing racks and fair trade goods. Defensible space is not just about discouraging certain behaviors or controlling activity; it's also about

Photo by Rajah Bose

The balcony view from inside the Community Building

inviting people to stay. That happened in the Community Building. We got that right.

In the Saranac Building, we still have challenges with defensible space. The lobby of the building is narrower and acts more like a hallway. We thought that adding a courtyard would help, but it didn't get used as much as we expected. As a result, that's where much of the unwanted activity has taken place in our buildings. Since no one claimed the space, it became a backdoor of the entire campus, a place where people are more likely to convene for illicit behaviors. The comfy furniture had to be removed to disincentivize lingering in that space. In retrospect, we learned some lessons. If the Saranac offices would have faced outward, it would have solved the problem. Had the office near the Magic Lantern and restaurant been more visible, that would have helped. Instead, maintenance staff conduct more frequent walkthroughs to keep an eye on what's going on.

Sustainability

As an architect, one of the things I love about Leadership in Energy and Environmental Design (LEED) is how it encourages the character of old buildings to be preserved. There are a lot of challenges that come with retrofitting an old building with new technology, but it's also an exciting endeavor. We had several types of materials that could be reused and counted toward our LEED point goals.

In the Saranac Building, which is the only LEED Platinum building on campus, the old metal ceiling panels were so beautiful it would have been a shame to discard them. We could salvage them, use them for LEED points, and have a beautiful visual impact on the space as well. But many of the panels were damaged. That's when I had the idea of taking and refurbishing as many of the panels as we could. We had enough for the main Saranac lobby. Then we eliminated the typical two-by-two gridded ceiling tiles in the Magic Lantern Theatre lobby and replaced them with some of the salvaged metal tiles, which completely transformed the lobby's atmosphere. We also saved the coved trim pieces and re-assembled them in the main entry hall of the Saranac.

The building required all new mechanical and electrical services. The only way to accommodate this new infrastructure was to run it along the tall existing ceilings—not exactly the visual impact we were going for. So, we reinstalled the refurbished, coved, ceiling trim on the walls, just below the space required for the new systems. We then floated the refurbished, metal, ceiling panels into a makeshift ceiling grid. We also added lighting above the floating panels so it would shine on the coved trim and emphasize it. It's a beautiful treatment—a great way to hide the necessary systems for the building while also providing a strong visual impression.

Light turned out to be an important part of making the building warm and inviting and obtaining a high LEED score. Our first go-around with lighting was efficient but very commercial. Recessed lighting everywhere just didn't fit the warm vibe we were going for. We had all these ceiling lights from the old Magic Lantern space and decided to convert them into wall sconces. That little experiment in repurposing gave us a whole new sense of what lighting could be.

On the second and fourth floors, we installed pendant lights from a church that was upgrading their lighting. I thought they would be a cool addition to the hallways, which don't need to be blasted with as much intense light because they don't serve as public spaces, and fewer tenants occupy them. In hallways, you just need enough light to maneuver around. This lowered light level made the hallways a comfortable transition space from the more brightly lit offices. This is the kind of creative workaround we were inspired to try because of LEED. Otherwise, we would have done the easy, automatic thing: purchased lights rather than reimagining and refurbishing them from another space.

The most recent project Jim and I collaborated on together opened in 2016. The Saranac Commons—which sits adjacent to the Community and Saranac Buildings—introduced a host of new challenges, while also allowing us to apply all we had learned about adaptive reuse. In the past, we had focused on creating beautiful spaces for nonprofits, but this was a commercial space focused on building community by investing in beauty *and* small businesses.

We wanted to create an inclusive, multi-use, multi-vendor space where people who work and live downtown can gather, and people visiting Spokane can sample local cuisine and feel welcome. We envisioned a similar aesthetic: natural light, repurposed materials, and intentional design to evoke positive emotions and thereby enhance the quality of connection for everyone who walks through the spacious roll-up front door.

Jim's team sent out a request for proposal, and we also listened to people on the block and folks who sent ideas via word of mouth. The mix of tenants didn't arise from a specific concept; rather, the concept was informed by the mix of tenants: two restaurants, a brewery, a bakery, a coffee shop, and a dried good store.

Although we did not seek the costly and time-consuming LEED certification in this project, we designed it with similar principles in mind. The building had beautiful old trusses, beams, skylights, and a lot of brick that could be exposed. Jim had initially imagined doing something like the Melrose Market in Seattle, but that space was much larger with higher ceilings, so they were able to do a lot with volume. Our challenge became, how do you arrange everything on one level and achieve a spacious, open, thriving feeling? We also didn't have a lot of room for storefront visibility and wondered how to give each of the individual tenants a presence. Who was going to be in the back, who was going to be in the front, how much non-visible space was needed for each?

The key was designing a space that people felt compelled to walk into, and creating a good circulation path so they naturally wandered all the way through.

Downtown Revitalization and Historic Preservation

Even for the buildings that were not on the historical registry, Jim wanted to preserve their integrity as much as possible, as a way to honor the existing neighborhood and the buildings' history.

While historic preservation was important, it was not the highest value on the list, and our approach to it was unconventional. We enhanced the essence of the building, but not for the sake of historic preservation itself. For example, we kept the core layout on the second and third floors with minimal intrusions. We kept the integrity of the hallways. Instead of tearing it down, we used an old building, which allowed us to focus on integrity, recycling, caring, preserving. The historical part was an added benefit. Really, we celebrated reuse and repurpose to stimulate, support, and inspire community. Jim could have torn buildings down. But the intent was to revitalize and create life. Restoration was a truer, more dynamic statement about what's happening here, about what community building looks like.

Because we were already working in this mode, getting on the historic registry was not a lot of extra effort. It mostly meant taking care of what was already there, preserving the original context—the face of the building and anything that's visible. We kept the Saranac's double-hung windows for this reason. We kept the matrix intact to maintain a historic feel. We didn't want to modernize or change anything unnecessarily. In some places, we preserved more than we had to. Most floors of the Saranac Building are still divided into their original small spaces because of historic connection to single-room occupancy. We could have expanded the mezzanine in the Community Building into a whole second floor, but we would have lost something interesting and original in the process.

You can think about this in contrast to other spaces around town. Before the Bank of America went in, an old Art Deco building stood in its place. Everything about it—the inside, the outside, all the materials—was beautiful, full of history, craftsmanship, and character. They tore it down, and they built the Bank of America, which is totally void of energy. Really. Walk into the Bank of America lobby and tell me how you feel. It's cold. Everything is granite or some other very hard surface. The color palette is light and bright. The lighting is intense. And it was built by people who weren't from Spokane, so it got plopped down in the middle of downtown with no concern for the local context.

When you renovate a building, you increase all the vitalism that's already there. While new builds are often about developers making their own statement, renovation has the power to enrich an existing history—for all of us. When a neighborhood has a strong, local context, the whole environment has strength.

In choosing to renovate old, neglected buildings in a long-neglected area of town, Jim and other business owners have created a nucleus of energy and vitalism in Spokane. This kind of energy and renewal extends beyond the walls of a building. I've seen this approach to development help renew the urban fabric of a town that previously felt dead on the outskirts. The new energy is contagious. Other property owners on our block have also been inspired to work with existing buildings and strived to use recycled materials. The result is something unique. It's not sterilized. It's an experience worth supporting. And while it's based on the old neighborhood format, it's still flexible enough to keep evolving.

CHAPTER FOUR

Beneath the Surface: Green Building Practices

By Austen White

Austen is the master tinkerer and green technology lead at the CBC. He has also served his country as an Air Force mechanic, performed wildfire fuels reduction in the Pacific Northwest, and managed operations at Holden Village.

When people ask what my job is, I say I fix things. Somebody else designs the buildings and puts systems in place. It's my job to maintain them, or perhaps, at the right time, to improve on them a little bit. I often think of the Buddhist Samurai temples in Japan. The temples have stood for thousands of years, and each generation's job is to keep the temples as they were. I like the idea of continuance, of honoring what came before me and caring for what continues after me. I want to honor the original design and intent of the buildings, and I honor the intent by keeping things working like they're supposed to.

Thanks to a varied background, I have always been in the position of learning new things. I've worked in construction, as a mechanic for a landscape company, a drywall delivery truck driver, as a heavy equipment mechanic at a Lutheran retreat center, and pitched in on trail crews and forest fuel-reduction through AmeriCorps. I also served for four years in the Air National Guard as a KC-135 mechanic. I was responsible for tearing apart tankers and airplanes. Every so many flight hours they have to be inspected. We'd bring them into the hangers, pull the panels off, and physically run our fingers along thousands of miles of cable to feel for burns and points that needed lubrication. We assigned discrepancies to various repair shops. Maybe the common threads through all of these jobs are patience, a willingness to keep trying until something works, and knowing when to ask for help if it doesn't or you're in over your head.

I was hired at the Community Building Campus in 2010 to train workers and oversee maintenance. Over the years, my job has shifted to more of an infrastructure maintenance position. It takes a lot of time and money to keep up with sustainable technologies. New advancements are being made all the time, which requires problem solving and decision-making. When should you upgrade? What is the most materials-efficient way to make those upgrades? How do you integrate new technologies into existing systems? After making the initial investment into sustainable technologies, how do you keep maintaining the system in a way that's congruent with the desire to be green in the first place? There is no guidebook for any of this. We're always trying, learning, failing, course correcting, and trying again.

When the Community and Saranac Buildings were in the design stage, sustainability was not a common design lens in Eastern Washington. The Community Building was the first community solar installation our local energy company, Avista, had ever done. There was a learning curve for both building management and Avista. But we worked well together, and they came back to study our solar arrays to better understand how we tie into the grid. They are interested in what we're doing because we're leading the local movement toward solar in the commercial space. I'm interested in what they're doing because how they manage their resources affects both commercial and residential users, the environment, and our community.

One of the reasons I make an effort to maintain this relationship is that I'd love to see Avista promote solar in commercial spaces. Right now, they are determining what their power mix will look like for the next twenty years. They've looked to us as a model in terms of both conservation and production. I hope they follow through on that interest and that we can help influence their energy mix toward greater efficiency. One of the challenges they face in both encouraging people to conserve energy and to invest in solar is that the region's power source is cheap. Hydroelectric energy in Washington State is some of the cheapest in the country. It's hard to incentivize people to conserve because

The Community Building Campus's green technology lead, Austen White

it won't save them much money. That's why it's so important to have examples out there like the Saranac Building. It's one thing to tell customers about it. It's another to see it in action. When people see our solar panels, they get excited, they get curious, they want to know the story, and they want to know if they can pull off solar, too.

Our solar arrays have historically taken up a lot of my time and attention and have brought the most opportunities to connect with other commercial spaces about green energy. Solar in urban, commercial spaces provides a lot of benefits that don't play out in residential settings because commercial generally uses energy as it is produced. In the summer, we're cooling the buildings in the middle of the day, which is also when the solar production is at its max. In a home, if you're gone at work when the system is producing the majority of its power, that power has to be exported somewhere else, and you lose some of your production. In commercial solar, you're almost never producing a glut of energy. You always use it where you produce it. One of my goals is to help press more commercial owners downtown to buy into solar, since they'll carry the biggest impact.

I've had a lot of folks ask for advice. We even offered a workshop that was well-attended, and two of the attendees ended up installing solar on their houses. However, I've been surprised at how resistant commercial building owners have been to the idea of solar. Interest hasn't materialized and state solar incentives have dwindled. It's also hard to convince business owners to make a thirty-year investment. I get it. Business owners have so many pressing needs that energy efficiency is often a last priority. Solar has to be part of a business owner's philosophy; otherwise, people see it as a complicated investment with minimal economic return that could potentially generate more headaches.

A lot of the most important green technologies are hidden in the guts of the buildings, which not a lot of people see. Efficient toilets and basement rain catchment systems are not as sexy as solar arrays and rooftop gardens, but they play a huge part in making the Saranac Building one of the greenest commercial buildings in the state. For example, we harvest rainwater for multiple uses, like watering the living roof and plants around the building. We also use it to flush our toilets. Since we're not using city water to flush, we reduce power used to pump water from the ground. The amounts are small, but they add up.

We also harvest ground water from a creek that runs through the basement of the Saranac. This kind of ground water source is common in urban areas where topography was eliminated to create flat building surfaces. Many commercial buildings have to manage groundwater and look for ways to divert it by discharging it into the sewer. At the Saranac, we found an ingenious solution: capture it and use it to flush the toilets. As a result, we're not using potable water to dispose of human waste. More importantly, our catchment system serves as combined sewer overflows (CSO) tanks. In big rain and storm events, the city sewer system overflows and discharges into the river. The same thing can happen in the springtime during snowmelt. We can store this excess water in our tanks and slowly release it, which helps keep the system from becoming overburdened and keeps sewage out of the river.

Both visible and invisible features, such as solar arrays and groundwater catchment, speak to how building designers used the local context to inspire design. Although they might not have realized it at the time, this integration of the landscape in building design is from the biomimicry playbook. I've been inspired by biomimicry principles when thinking about the lifespan of a building. The Saranac hosted its grand opening in 2007, which means that the systems in our buildings are now thirteen years old. We are already starting in on big infrastructure improvement projects, such as solving some problems with bacterial build-up in our wells.

Often, we see the aging-out of building components as a negative thing. Especially with large buildings, we start to feel like everything is breaking down and showing wear. It's stressful because it takes time and costs money to perform upkeep. When managing a built environment, it's useful to think about buildings as having generations, just like life. In ecological succession, a biological community evolves over time. In applying succession principles to building management practices, we're always looking out for what's new, what's innovative—paying close attention to what's happening while simultaneously planning ahead. That way we can make incremental changes that maintain the optimum function of current systems while looking to integrate new technologies as they become viable and available.

For example, when Avista started offering incentives to switch from incandescent and fluorescent to LED, we took advantage of the program right away. As a result, we now conserve enough power—compared to our usage in 2011—to power 9.5 homes. In solar production, we produce roughly enough energy to power 5.5 homes, which means we gain twice as much power through conservation as we do from our solar production. I've brought this up with city council members because a lot—perhaps too much—attention is focused on how to produce more green energy. But conservation is by far a bigger payoff and produces faster results with less input. I've been trying to find time in my schedule to track these kinds of conservation measures and tell this story.

The opposite of a succession approach to building management is gutting a building every twenty years and replacing everything with newer, cheaper components. This is at times economical, but it's such a destructive, wasteful strategy. The other option is to ask a new question: Since we know we'll have to update or replace aging infrastructure, what can we do to make this inevitability more positive? We can start by thinking about what we have in place that does work and by looking at what doesn't need to be replaced. That's the kind of challenge I really enjoy. An example of this blend of old and new is our LED lighting, where we used adapters so that we could keep the casing and only replace the tubes. We opted to reuse existing housings as opposed to buying brand new fixtures.

Another example of conservation paying off is how the Main Market took advantage of Avista's rebate program. The market has custom pendant lighting,

The Saranac Building's solar array (2007)

and Avista was willing to do a special case exception for a commercial facility. It penciled out for both of us: Avista paid for the new LEDs, and we ended up using exactly half the energy the following year. An additional benefit is that the interior of the Main Market used to be dim, and the new lights are brighter, which is better for customers and workers. The new LED lights also have an added benefit in that they do not produce heat like the old incandescent bulbs. One problem is the disposal of the old bulbs, which we have to pay for. This is one huge problem with the energy code: there is no easy way or incentive to recycle the bulbs, even though legislation says we have to, which means a lot of these products are disposed of improperly.

Unfortunately, there's no guide for sustainable building management like there is for people who are trying to use real estate to accumulate wealth. Even in light of new technologies, sustainable building management is still a huge challenge, but it's in the same spirit as the challenges that Jim and his team confronted from the beginning. Since we seldom elect to proceed in a standardized way at the CBC, sometimes I wonder, does anything I'm doing make sense? But then I remember there hasn't been an easy blueprint in place from the beginning. The Saranac was an experiment in restoring a building from the ground up. The original management team had to keep in mind the historical context and existing structures while being imaginative about energy efficiency and cutting-edge technologies. Everything had to be matched and rethought. If something didn't quite work, then they tried something new. For example, one of the biggest challenges in the LEED certification was fitting all the piping for gray water flushing and roof irrigation. They dismantled the old tin ceiling tiles, installed the piping, and reinstalled the tiles as a beautiful, antique dropped ceiling.

The Saranac was not just an experiment in restoration, but also in promoting human health in a commercial environment. Thanks to LEED certification, we have strict ventilation standards. There are minimum ventilation standards for any commercial building, but this one goes above and beyond, making sure fresh air is present in every room at all times through CO_2 monitoring. Pumping fresh air into offices allows us to cool the building essentially for free. In the summer, anytime the building is warmer than the outside temperature, we pipe in cold air. This is called "free cooling" because it doesn't use any refrigeration or electricity other than fans. These ducts are one of the biggest structures installed during the renovation. To ventilate the building like they did, which has a positive impact on human health, required a lot of space. The LEED certification forced them to work as much as possible with what they had, and our job today is to continue that conversation with the building.

As proud as I am of these buildings, I understand why developers may want to avoid this kind of project. Although a lot of our systems are automated, they still require time and input. They have a lot of components, and all components have a lifespan. I'm constantly checking, calibrating, moving, and changing things. I've also had to acquire diverse skill sets, like computer languages, familiarity with software, and managing interactions with hardware.

The Saranac has the greenest features of any of the buildings on our campus. Some of them were cutting-edge technologies at the time of installation in 2007. For example, the Saranac had geothermal heating and cooling, which is available because we sit on a huge aquifer. Our ground source heat pump allowed us to utilize the earth's constant temperature of 52 degrees. In the summer we used this air to cool the buildings, and in winter we started heating air at 52 degrees rather than using the air outside the building that was much colder. We also have solar arrays on three of our buildings and three rooftop gardens that provide insulation, deflect heat, expand the life of roofing materials, and add beauty to our outdoor spaces.

Because of the unique nature of the geothermal system we designed, we also had unique problems. Certain bacteria that live in the ground thrive in iron-rich environments. When steel well casings are driven into the ground, these bacteria begin to flourish in their new environment. Unfortunately, the waste products produced by these bacteria are extremely acidic and cause rapid corrosion of the plumbing components. We hired commercial well cleaners to decrease the bacterial sludge, and new pipes and pumps were installed. These steps would typically resolve the issues, at least for an extended period. However, our system was uniquely designed to work on a single downtown parcel, and we ended up recycling our ground water along with the bacteria. After several attempts we were forced to abandon the geothermal wells in favor of an air-source heat pump system.

But even when we made the HVAC switch, it was important we didn't go the easy route. Because of our attempts to fix the geothermal system, we were bleeding money, and on one level it would have made sense to put in another boiler and submit to natural gas. However, we honored the original intent and installed a relatively new technology, a set of hydronic heat pumps to heat and cool the water formerly used in the geothermal wells. These decisions are not always linear, and we went through a painful process to find something that was a great match. But we didn't fully surrender to the problem. We found a solution that gave us credibility and that helps us reduce greenhouse gas.

Even when things are working well, our systems are more management intensive. For example, with irrigation and groundwater plumbing alone, there are three times as many plumbing systems to worry about. We have to work with specially trained contractors, and only a couple of people in Spokane can work on our HVAC. These are not set-it-and-forget-it systems. Many times, a lot of thought goes into planning a building, but not a lot goes into what happens once it's built. You have to be willing to monitor and make changes right off the bat, and to measure changes over time so that you can figure out how to get the most out of your systems. This input and management could be seen as negative, but I think it's great. We should be doing things that force us to think, learn, and adapt.

In this way, my work lines up with the work of our tenants, who are working to create greater change from a micro level, from the bottom up. So many people who work in the buildings are innovating and trying new approaches all the time. They are challenging and shifting current power structures. My role is to complement their work by maintaining a nice place where they can do their work. I facilitate that by making sure they can bring people to the

Photo by Jon Snyder

Jim Sheehan receiving the Saranac Building's LEED certification

space and breathe clean air and feel safe and comfortable. I'm always observing, changing, and trying to improve, and like them, I'm also striving for change on a regional or local level. It's easier to think about the macro scale, or change from the top down, because you don't have to be as interactive as you would on an individual, person-to-person level. Policy that forces people to adopt certain behaviors can change rapidly from administration to administration. But starting from the bottom up creates more lasting benefits because you're working with people to find solutions, not just forcing them to change their minds. Just like producing food locally, producing energy locally uses fewer resources. Changing minds locally is incredibly powerful because not only do you make change, but you also become partners. You build community through effecting change.

I've seen other commercial buildings that are as beautiful as the buildings on the CBC. I can think of a really cool corporate campus I visited that takes up two city blocks. The office building is in the center, and it has a massive campus with green spaces, natural areas, and tennis courts. But the lawn is highly manicured, deep green, and uses a ton of water. The campus is neat, but it's a classic definition of beauty, the same green lawns you've seen a thousand times, with the sprinklers always going. I see the intent, but it's hard for me to see beauty when there's waste.

What I like about the Community Building Campus is that it has a different kind of beauty. Not just flashy, surface-level features like eye-catching green spaces or fountains, but a resilient kind of beauty where preservation and having a low profile and hidden features is beautiful. I think this approach is subtler and more modern. The Community Building Campus shows that making a truly beautiful building doesn't have to harm the environment—maybe just your pocketbook a little bit. I'd like to see us change our expectations of beauty to include important ideas like conservation. The Community Building is a great argument for this kind of space: one that is beautiful outside and in.

CHAPTER FIVE

Coordinating Community

By Dave Sanders

Dave started as the general contractor for the Saranac and Community Building renovations before transitioning to the community coordinator role, where he supported operations and tenant relations. Now retired, he is proud of, and grateful for, years well spent.

I came to Spokane from Walla Walla for the World's Fair. Expo '74, as it's now known, was the first large-scale attempt to clean up the core feature of downtown, the Spokane Falls and riverfront, which was choked by train tracks, warehouses, and industrial refuse. I was hired to work for a drop-in counseling center, a job created from some of the World's Fair funding to deal with any drug crisis on the fairgrounds next to the Spokane River. Fortunately, drug overdoses were very rare, and we ended up looking for lost children more than anything else.

I loved being right in the heart of downtown. Our office was around the corner from what would become the Community Building. The Saranac Building had a little grocery run by a Korean lady, and to my memory the rest of the businesses were secondhand stores. Within a few blocks there were a lot of little places to eat—counter and stool-style places that were user-friendly and affordable. I remember Stan's Coney Island and Mother's Kitchen. When the fair went away, I stayed on for a year doing direct counseling, where I managed a group in the jail and on-call drug crisis management at the hospital. When I got married, the work was too much of an emotional drain, and so I started working construction.

In high school, my friends knew they were going to be lawyers, superintendents to schools, or doctors, but I didn't know what I wanted to do. I worked in counseling and construction, among other kinds of jobs, but I never forgot about a dream I had in high school. I saw myself turning fifty years old and getting involved with a wellness center project. I didn't know how I would get there, or even what a wellness center was, exactly. I thought it might manifest as a retreat space, where staff, corporations, boards of directors, or nonprofits could come when they needed to do training, and that it could also be used for family gatherings, teaching parenting skills, or anything else the community needed. When I saw what Jim was investing in at the Community Building Campus, I thought, well maybe that's it. The Community Building really is for the health of the whole human being.

I got involved in the project as a contractor with my business partner, Ron Peacock. My wife, Lynne, who passed away from cancer in 2014, was also invited with Anita Morgan (Chapter 8) to create and grow the Community Building Children's Center. My previous career in counseling came in handy because at that end of town we would see some of the famous street people I met and worked with at the drop-in center—people like Mumbles who had a photographic memory and talked unintelligibly to himself while he rapidly turned the pages of a magazine, or Spinner, who had Tourette's and whirled around in circles as he shouted unusual phrases.

That part of town used to be one of the primary social service areas in Spokane. Just before we started renovations, the old Salvation Army building on Division and Main was condemned, and the Rescue Mission one block up on Spokane Falls Boulevard built a new facility on Trent. But Main Avenue was still a familiar space to the people who hung out there, and lots of formerly homeless people lived in the decrepit apartments above a few of the bars. Most of them were gentle people, but a few were the type I wouldn't want to meet alone in the alley. However, we were able to maintain civil relationships with most of these folks and treat them as members of the downtown community.

As we finished up the Community Building Annex, I informed my business partner I was planning to leave. I had started taking classes in organizational leadership at Gonzaga University. I wanted to become a community organizer. But before getting started, Jim approached me about taking on a community coordinator position on the campus, and I took that position instead. The title was a catch-all for everything I wanted to do and all that needed to be done. I gave myself two primary tasks: invest in the culture of the Community Building spaces and organize the individuals and businesses on our block so we could work toward enhancements and improvements together.

We had to start by organizing within. When I came on as community coordinator, the Community Building lacked daily leadership. Jim was spending a lot of the time running a ranch and retreat with his new wife in California. The guy who was acting as operations manager at the time didn't have much training and struggled with the politics of the space. There were some really strong personalities and opinions, and he got run over a bit by the competing interests of two factions: the Center for Justice, whose members thought they best represented Jim's interest, and all the other tenants, who also felt a deep sense of ownership of the space. In some ways, this conflict made sense to me because no one really knew what the culture of the space was going to be. Jim had set everything in motion, but he wasn't available to participate in the daily operations and relationship management. The space didn't need a traditional hierarchical structure, which Jim and many of the organizations actively opposed, but it did need someone to invest in the culture and facilitate the interactions that would keep the place running.

The open-ended objective of the Community Building—to build community—meant the space could evolve based on the needs of the tenants and the greater community. But it also meant that organizations naturally arrived with assumptions that lingered. For example, there was an assumption on some tenants' part that ultimately the building would be under their ownership, that the legal structure would transfer to a cooperative ownership that would last for perpetuity. Many of them had come from a failed nonprofit center just north of the city. It was set up in a similar way, but it collapsed when the main guy who owned it died. Tenants were skittish from that experience. Plus, everyone carried the daily expectations that all people have: those thoughts, feelings, and desires that come with being human.

Back when we were doing renovations on the building, I also wondered if eventually the project would come under tenant ownership. Jim seemed to want as much community buy-in as possible, and transferring the legal responsibility over to tenants, in addition to declaring the buildings as the community's space like he already had, seemed like an interesting idea. Now, however, I'm glad we didn't do that. It makes more sense for tenants to focus on their missions

Dave Sanders supported the CBC's operations and tenant relations

and their daily work in the community and let someone else take care of the buildings. It's a lot of responsibility and a lot of voices to manage when decisions about one-ply vs. two-ply toilet paper are being made democratically. For a time, we invited tenants to participate in some of the more minute responsibilities, but it took away from their ability to collaborate on other levels. If we came together in a group meeting or people served together on a board, talk about what kind of toilet paper they were going to buy inevitably crept in. The building operations team decided to just take care of the property management so that the tenants could focus on what really matters.

What really mattered to me was creating a collegial atmosphere. I hoped that people would recognize that there were enough resources to go around, and people didn't have to compete for them. Many of these organizations were small, one- or two-person offices, and they were all scrambling for money. In some respects, they were even going after the same grant money, although they each had different mission statements. But they were competing for the same livelihood in the sense that grant dollars are limited, and funding sources are always insecure since they could change based on the whims of legislatures or the economy. But by giving them reduced rents—all they had to pay were the utilities, some taxes, and cleaning fees—we were giving them the conditions where they could relax, focus on their work, and collaborate more. Unfortunately, some individuals came in with so much baggage that they had a hard time leaning into the new system we were trying to create.

One of the first things I did was invite people from each floor who had frequent concerns to form an executive council. Five or six of us met once a month to voice concerns, and we focused on defining what consensus meant. For us, it meant that even if you don't agree with an approach, we find one everyone can at least live with. Having a time and place set aside to talk about the ongoing struggles of living in community was important. The philosophy of most organizations in the buildings was that everyone should be heard, but the organizations themselves didn't have anyone to listen to them. I decided that part of my leadership was being that person.

I also had an open-door policy for all organizations. Anyone could stop by if they needed something. I would also make rounds on a regular basis. I would get out of my office and see people, just to check in. I loved going in and talking to people and having a cup of coffee. Sometimes we chatted about Community Building issues, but a lot of times we talked about challenges within their own organizations. When a conflict would arise in an organization with only a couple employees, then a staff member might have no one to take their complaint or concern to. I often listened to HR-related issues without weighing in—just to be supportive and help people process their concerns. In an informal way, I was doing HR work. But more than anything else, it was what I've come to call relational counseling. I tried to be there for people and give them somewhere at work where they could talk their troubles out. This sharing of self goes back to the wellness of the individual. When you come clean, and are able to come as who you are, then it's easier to have compassion. When you can release some of the emotional weight of human troubles, it's easier to work for the common good.

Sometimes I facilitated conversations about building-wide concerns. One stands out because it was highly personal and yet so many people got involved. There was one woman who was skittish about walking through the stairwell alone because she had been attacked at some point in her life. She approached me about putting mirrors in the stairwell, but somehow her personal concern escalated into pro-mirror versus anti-mirror campaigns. The pro-mirror side's position was yes, you need to install mirrors because it's the right thing to do so that this woman feels safe. The anti-mirror side decided to speak for Jim and say no; he wouldn't want mirrors. Mirrors feel too much like surveillance, and Jim's not a surveillance kind of guy. So, I invited everyone to come together. We went through a process where everyone was invited to speak, but the rule was you could only speak for yourself. You could not say what you thought someone else wanted or needed. This situation required more nuance than a lot of the issues we handled, such as what kind of soap we should use in the bathrooms or whether one-ply or two-ply toilet paper was more environmentally friendly. Having people come together to discuss an issue that impacted her made the woman feel more secure, like a whole building full of people had her back. It was an example of the collective paying attention, caring for an individual, and trying to take ownership of each other.

I always hoped we would come together as a group, and I think by the end of my first two years, we did that well. At the very least we had cultivated a live and let live sense, an understanding that, if someone needed help, or if something about being in the Community Building was stressful for them, they had a person like me who they could turn to help solve the problem. Quarterly potlucks were also an important part of bringing people together. Getting together just for the sake of getting together—without a formal meeting agenda; just to check in on and be with each other—was one of the best things we did.

When I first started that position, I told Jim, "If I'm successful at what I want to do, I'll be out of a job." I thought that within around two years, I would be able to get enough culture building done that there would be no need for me anymore. But two things happened: first, we realized that the work of culture building is ongoing and that it would never end. Secondly, Jim purchased another building, the old Hotel Saranac, with the intention of expanding the Community Building project. He would need someone to stay on as we doubled our square footage and brought more than twice as many organizations into the fold.

I was a little concerned when we went from just the Community Building to adding the Saranac. All of a sudden, we brought in about seventy-five new people, and the new group was larger than the existing group. I decided that we needed to name and be intentional about this shift. So, we booked a local retreat site and did a workshop with a facilitator. The biggest message I got out of it was life was kind of messy, and we bring that messiness to work with us because we are people, and that's OK. I remember it was a beautiful spring day, and we got mixed up pretty well and got to know each other. But the long-term impact of the retreat was something I didn't learn about until later. People who attended this retreat and still work on campus refer to it as one of their favorite CBC occasions. Although few of us can remember the content, we remember the experience of being together, of feeling supported in our pursuits as individuals and in our struggles to make Spokane a city where more people could experience justice.

Adding the Saranac into the mix did more than change the interpersonal dynamics on campus. We got more press and more attention at the Saranac than the Community Building because of how we were renovating it. The LEED Platinum certification, which was a nightmare to manage and added huge costs to the project, was worth it in the long run. A lot of the requirements for earning extra points to obtain the Platinum certification were beyond what's really feasible or practical for a lot of projects. But Jim was proud to have the largest private solar array in Eastern Washington because he wanted to set an example so that more entrepreneurs and developers would start integrating sustainable technologies into their building practices. The project also increased our credibility in the city. We had a much larger physical footprint, and the cutting-edge technologies were really interesting to people.

Soon after the Saranac opened, the city was going through a bond-rating process, and they were trying to get the bond rates lowered. The City employees brought the actuaries up to the rooftop gardens, which have a lovely view of downtown and are also a great vantage point for viewing our solar arrays. They said, this is the kind of thing that's happening in the City of Spokane. They used the optics of the Community Building, from the beautiful aesthetic to the work on social concerns, to basically say, we are a great, progressive city! Don't we deserve to have our bond rates lowered in 2009? I don't know what the outcome was for the city, but I liked that our hard work was being recognized, and that we were helping set a standard for what Spokane could become.

In the end I stayed for twelve years, in part because we kept acquiring new buildings. I decided to stay because I loved the work and felt like I was making a difference in people's lives. After we got through that initial two-year period and started becoming cohesive as a group, I also began focusing on having a voice within the city and within the Downtown Spokane Partnership.

It was good timing to start planting seeds. The Downtown Spokane Partnership, which was formerly the chamber of commerce, had a woman, Marty Dickenson, who wasn't as entrenched in the good ol' boys club. She was more interested in cultivating the vision of what the city could look like, and she was really receptive to new ideas. Most of the influence on the direction of downtown Spokane came from people with narrowly focused business interests. I showed up at meetings to represent the little shops that at this point had been left out of most conversations about the direction for the city. We talked about how to get more people downtown, what that looks like, and how to get more business on the sidewalk. We also talked about making Main Street a two-way street. The design ethic of previous decades focused on efficiency for automobile transit and parking. As a result, downtown Spokane included lots of one-way streets that served as corridors to get cars from the highway to parking garages and back to the highway as quickly as possible. We wanted to advocate for the return of a two-way Main Avenue, for traffic-calming measures, and for the restoration of neighborhoods and historic districts. As we built relationships in the city, we started reaching out to our other neighbors and had community meetings. We also had our own conversations about what we wanted our neighborhoods to look like, and how to make that grow. We were one small group in a larger community, and I tried to make our voices heard. It's hard to keep news about community, city priorities, and social justice to yourself, and I tried to plant these seeds around the city through relationships. We didn't accomplish a lot of this in my tenure at the CBC, but when Rebecca Mack (Chapter 2) took on this work after I left, they finally started seeing some movement.

Looking back, I realize I didn't have a manual for my community coordinator position. I relied on my background in counseling and my relational strengths to help me intuit my way through. I relied heavily on my understanding of community organizing models, which bring people together to think more deeply about what they want. In this way of working together, it's important to get to the root of an issue, at what it is people actually need. Someone might say, for example, "Well, I want a light outside my house." Well, what does a light get you? Is that for security, or so that your kids can play soccer after dark? What is it that you really want from that light? Once you know why they want the light, a conversation can start about deeper concerns and better problem solving.

Although it can be time consuming to always be in conversation, it's really the only way to move forward together as a community. We didn't want to destroy what we had already developed. We didn't want to force any kind of change, no matter how small. If you force change, you're not committed to the larger vision of building community and investing in relationships, and the relationships are the most important component of the whole project.

CHAPTER SIX

Building Stewardship

By Warrin Bazille

Warrin has served as a building and relationship steward for fifteen years and counting. He's the first to arrive in the morning and the first to pitch in when something unexpected comes up.

When people walk into our buildings, they generally look up at the high ceilings, the exposed brick, and the natural light. But when I get to work early each morning, I usually find myself looking *down*, gauging the cleanness of the floors that I've stripped and refinished several times over. The first twenty to thirty minutes of my day is usually a walkthrough of the buildings to make sure everything is running, that heat pumps and mechanical equipment are functioning properly, and that there are no leaks or other big problems. I've done these morning walkthroughs so often over the last fifteen years that I don't even need a checklist.

In the early morning, it's quiet, so if I'm sealing floors, working on a toilet, or fixing a light, I can get a lot done. When we open the buildings at 7 a.m., everything changes. I still spend my day observing and working on the physical needs of the buildings, but I spend a lot of time on other kinds of stewardship, too. The most important part of my job is interacting with tenants around the buildings and pausing for conversations. I always try to be a good listener because I get a lot from lifting people up and encouraging them. They may be going through a storm, and being greeted with a big ol' smile can remind them that sunshine and clear skies are coming ahead. I see little moments with people not as interruptions in my job and routine, but part of what I can contribute. I try to bring a spirit of love to these day-to-day interactions.

For years, we offered a training program for young men and women from challenged families and broken homes. David Edwards (another long-time CBC employee) and I wanted to build their skills through hands-on training and get these young people ready for employment. It takes a lot of time and energy to train and coach, but David had a special gift. He was good at stepping into chaotic homes and communicating with troubled youth and their parents. Many of the young people had criminal histories, some with felonies, or as David said, "an F on their backs." David recognized that without help, their opportunities would be limited.

We worked as a team to build attitudes along with confidence and skills so that they could be more employable. We taught them painting, sheet rocking, plumbing, waxing, and floor maintenance. We did projects like building new basement stairs so they could learn framing and basic carpentry. Then we organized classroom sessions so we could teach them the basics: how to read a tape measure, how to calculate diameter and circumference, how much weight is OK on a two by four. We gave them opportunities to learn, grow, and be gainfully employed, even with the hard knock of a criminal record. I've run into some of them years later as managers at Costco or employees at Caterpillar. Some of them had already been in jail when they started with us, so it was rewarding to see them go out and find a good stable job.

I know what it's like to need some extra support—we all do—and I was lucky enough to get that from my family. I grew up between Seattle (where my mom lived) and Houston (where my dad lived). When I was in Houston, I spent a lot of time at Grandma Iona's house when my dad had to work. We come from a big family down south. Grandma Iona had sixteen kids, and now with grandkids, in-laws, and greats, there's around one hundred and twenty of us. I remember she wore jeans when harvesting tomatoes in the garden, and she put her hair in rollers and wore beautiful dresses for church on Sunday. Her hair was naturally curly, and she often wore it down, a cascading symbol of her Native American and African American heritage. She taught us the values of being kind, treating people with respect, and also that your word meant something. On Sundays, a lot of us came together. There would be thirty of us, eating at tables set up in the yard. We talked, played football, and made music.

Warrin Bazille, steward of CBC's buildings and relationships for over fifteen years

Sunday dinners were always big. Grandma Iona made biscuits that sat up three to four inches. She prepared fried fish, fried chicken, baked chicken, or BBQ. She also made six to seven side dishes like mac 'n cheese, collard greens, black-eyed peas, or candied yams. I was the youngest one in the house with my grandma, and I helped her in the kitchen a lot. If I was in there, I was able to eat. I'd say, we need to test this, Grandma. She'd say, you can be the tester, baby. I would clean the bowls for cakes before they got to the dishwasher. Now, Grandma Iona is ninety-six years old, and she takes care of the grandkids still. I called her not long ago and asked, "Can you give me a recipe for the biscuits? Mine aren't coming out right." She said, "Baby, you just have to keep practicing," which is exactly how she came to make perfect biscuits. She has really been the glue of the family, and her values still stand today.

I went to church a lot. My dad was Catholic, grandmother was Baptist, and my mother was Pentecostal. I grew up in Catholic school, praying in the morning and afternoon, where services were short. At Baptist church, they were long sermons. At the Pentecostal church, we were just dancing. Growing up in different faith communities helped me understand there are a lot of ways to love people. It's why I try to treat the people who aren't tenants just as well as the people who come to work here every day. I see every encounter as the chance to show people the love of God. Through all the religions, God really talks about a lot of forgiveness, being humble, and loving your neighbor.

When I train new people, I always tell them: we are not security, we are stewards. We're more like gardeners who talk to the people who come in to enjoy the garden. The way we manage the buildings is very communication-intensive. We do our work differently here than other buildings around town. Our job is to help people find resources or whatever they may need, almost like a concierge service. If visitors come into the building for another reason, like to get into some kind of trouble, we tell them we are there to keep them and everyone else safe. We are greeters, we are resources, we are safety officers. Every now and then we may have to escort someone off the property and ask them to leave, but for the most part our interactions are more nuanced.

My friendship with George best demonstrates this approach. George was one of the first people I met when I started at the Community Building in 2005. He lived in the shelter beside the building, which was located where the Saranac Pub now is. He used to come over and sit with us when we were eating lunch or working on the building. George always smiled big and said to me, "Hey Big W, how you doing?" I'd say, "Man, you remind me of Sylvester Stallone in flannel." He had a deep voice, muscled-up body, and black hair. We helped George out, sometimes financially with a meal or a coat. And when a group of us walked to the Westminster Congregational Church to take an AA meeting every week, he would go with us.

George knew the neighborhood because he lived there back when the Saranac Building was a single-room occupancy hotel. He showed me around the building before it was rebuilt. George and I went through floor by floor, and he shared all the information of what happened: who worked here, who got killed here, who did the maintenance back then. He told me about the past, which helped me get ready for the future. I was new to the neighborhood, and George knew everyone who was in transition at the men's shelter. If we needed some help escorting someone off the premises, he was there to help with that, too. Nights in the alley in those days could be scary, and we had the stress of protecting the kids in the daycare during the day, which was next door to the men's shelter. George taught me that how I approached the situation was the most important thing. I learned over time to be nice. *Hello, how's it going? Can I get you a cup of coffee?* I know it doesn't work for all people, but it does for some.

We were confronted with a whole different set of challenges when Jim Sheehan first started developing on the block. Back then, there was a lot of drinking, swearing, and guys hanging out. Although homeless services are no longer next door, we've seen a lot more drug usage in the homeless population that passes through or hangs out on the block. A lot of the places where people access resources have their hands full. They are challenged because of finances and the health hazards of the pandemic. There is now a greater demand on the public parts of our building, like the first-floor lobbies and bathrooms, but we still try to serve everyone by providing warmth, a friendly atmosphere, and by nurturing different people who come in for different resources. Despite ongoing hardships, it is still worth managing the buildings in this way. It's the only way we can follow through with our belief that everyone deserves a second chance, and that sometimes even when people have changed or cleaned themselves up, they still make mistakes.

We try to mitigate risk through relationship, but I also take care of security concerns in more traditional ways. For example, I'm still on them locks. I've been doing them for a long time and had no break-ins yet, ever. I do get calls at night when people are locked out or their codes aren't working, and sometimes I have to come down to meet tenants to let them in. With new technology coming along, we've been talking about key cards and are about to make some big changes on that front. But even with these traditional measures, there's a way to be personal and friendly. I've changed hundreds of locks through the years, which means that the first person a lot of people meet when they start as a new tenant in the building is me. I do the routine paint and clean-up of the office from the previous tenant, change out the old locks, and give the new tenant keys on the check in.

In addition to my employment on the CBC team, I got involved with a lot of other organizations as well. I helped the Center for Justice make Meals on Wheels deliveries to senior citizens. When a whole population of seniors was kicked out of their affordable housing unit, Sue Ellen at the Center for Justice worked the phones and her connections to find them apartments. Then other CBC staff and I loaned our time and trucks to help the seniors load their boxes and move. I attended NAACP meetings when the organization moved into the Community Building in 2015. I wasn't involved in leadership, but I sat and listened to everything. At the end, I offered my opinion about different situations. I helped Mark Gauthier at the Upper Columbia United Tribes (UCUT) with a

A view inside the Saranac Commons, complete with gleaming floors

Photo by Rajah Bose

film he was working on called *Gulf Coast Blues: Oil in Our Veins.* He knew I had roots in Louisiana, and he asked me background questions as part of his research and then on camera as one of the interviewees. CMTV recruited me to be a part of their commercials and community surveys on healthcare. The Northwest Fair Housing Alliance asked me to serve as one of their housing applicants, which helped them identify discrimination in the community. I helped with events in the Community Building lobby, like the Peace and Justice Action League of Spokane, creating an art installation that lined the room with the boots of soldiers killed in the second Iraq War. I helped with fair trade bazaars where we packed the space with abundant goods from around the world.

My involvement with so many different organizations shows me every day how tenants and CBC staff all work together to make the world a better place. I have experienced this compassion and support personally on many different occasions, and especially over these last few years. There's been an increase in bold racism as different groups started coming out and being more active in Spokane. The racism I saw before was more discrete and unintentional, likely related to implicit biases. I've been on the block for fifteen years now, and after all the years I've been here, this is the first time individuals have targeted me and actively pursued me to try to make me uncomfortable, threaten me, or harm me. We've also had groups gather on our block, wave their guns, and yell in a threatening way, with the police nowhere to be found. I understand protests and freedom of speech, but you have to examine their intent. What was this gathering meant for? Was it intimidation? It certainly felt that way to me.

One of my co-workers and I both arrive at the CBC hours before the sun is up. I'm a Black man, and he is a refugee from Burma who spent years in a refugee camp in Thailand before getting his green card and coming to the United States. One day in 2017, he arrived to find doors of the buildings covered with white nationalist, antisemitic, and anti-refugee flyers. Tensions have been rising since then, and even on this block, where everyone is so kind, we have to look out for each other in a more intentional and pronounced way. Since we're the first ones on campus in the morning, we do a meet-up every day and call and check in with each other more regularly.

Still, overall, we're blessed. I felt loved by how my co-workers and neighbors responded to this increase of negativity on the block and across the city. Our co-workers and other people who worked on campus could see the tensions and felt our tenseness. They checked in to ask how it was going for me, and they were kind to us in both word and action. They made calls and encouraged public officials like State Representatives Timm Ormsby and Marcus Riccelli, who both have offices in the Saranac Building, to sign a public letter condemning the "presence of armed vigilantes" and "the tactics used to intimidate and put fear in the citizenry." When our coworker confronted those racist flyers, the CBC teamed up with Civic Dinners and invited everyone on campus to share a meal together and to discuss Martin Luther King Jr.'s idea of Beloved Community. These kinds of actions recognize that we can't all be at 100 percent all the time. If you're struggling, someone else says, well, I can help. That's community.

Just as important as the community coming together when things get tough is people gathering to celebrate each other. We've done this in so many ways over the years, and I have the pleasure of preparing a lot of the food on these occasions. I think these events tell a lot about us. The food we cook up and share shows we are a team. Every Christmas season the CBC staff hosts a holiday party for everyone in the buildings. I cook the turkeys and hams, and tenants bring the sides. I also grilled all the food when staff hosted the annual Community Building Soccer Camp for kids at a nearby park. One of my favorite activities was closing down the block and hosting a lot of street fairs over the years. I brought out my trailer and grilled up food for these occasions, too. Organizations from the buildings set up tables and shared with the public what they do and what they're about. We had bands, a DJ, a big stage, and dancing in the street. Sometimes Jim even got behind the mic for a few minutes to talk about the mission of the campus and invite everyone to participate. The community was really healthy. What I mean by healthy is everyone knew each other and there were a lot of close relationships.

These days it's a little broader. Lots of people are moving into the neighborhood, and they haven't networked yet. Everyone is going the same way, making Spokane a better place, but they are in different lanes. As the campus has grown bigger over the years, sometimes people are not as close because they don't know each other. But when we team up to help one another, to confront hate in personal and public ways, I know that this place is still working. That's why the networking part of my job is more important than ever. I'm still the grill master at our summer BBQs, and when I see people, I always ask the same ol' questions: "Have you met? Let me introduce you." From there, it just opens up. I intentionally help people build relationships. Everyone who works on the campus, and especially CBC staff, are the glue, like my Grandma Iona, constantly working to bring people together in that original spirit of love.

CHAPTER SEVEN

The Rise and Sunset of the Center for Justice

By Breean Beggs

Breean is a social-change lawyer who served as the first executive director of the Center for Justice and is now the president of Spokane's City Council. He is leading efforts to increase affordable housing and sustainability while facilitating conversations on equity and inclusion.

The story of how I stepped into the role of chief catalyst/executive director of the Center for Justice in 2004 starts at a classic hamburger joint: the Clayton Drive-In Restaurant on Highway 395, just north of Spokane. My law firm in Bellingham specialized in cross-border accidents, and I had just finished a court argument near Colville, a few miles from the Canadian border. My college roommate's family had owned the drive-in, and I stopped in to order a banana milkshake. I noticed a copy of *The Spokesman-Review*, thumbed through it, and discovered an article about the Center for Justice.

I happened to be teaching a class in a law and diversity program to help disadvantaged undergraduate students prepare for law school, and I knew some of my students wanted to go to Gonzaga. Once back in Bellingham, I told my students about the Center for Justice and, sure enough, one of my students later attended Gonzaga Law School and interned at the Center for Justice. In October 2003, he sent me an email asking if I would be interested in applying for the executive director position, or if I knew anyone who would be.

I had always been drawn to public interest work and had pursued a fair amount of it in private practice, but there were limited jobs in that area of the law. I became a lawyer in 1991 in the wake of huge Reagan-era funding cuts to legal aid—free or discounted attorney representation in non-criminal cases for people who are at or near the poverty line—and there were fewer opportunities to do public service work full-time. This was especially true after Newt Gingrich's Contract with America, a 1994 legislative agenda that waged a war on legal aid and, therefore, waged war on equal access to justice for all. Gingrich also helped engineer restrictions for federally funded legal aid lawyers. Essentially, you weren't allowed to file class action lawsuits, assist people who were undocumented or incarcerated, or do much work on cases where attorneys' fees were available, which typically helps fund future work in legal aid.

So, when I had the chance to work at the Center for Justice, I was hopeful and optimistic. The Center was unfettered by this political chaos and had funding to do meaningful work that was being slashed by federal channels. It was liberating to be able to come to a place and say, my job every day is to do justice.

At that time, the Center was still searching for its identity in the community and—based on the interests of the attorneys who worked there—was essentially an alternative legal aid center. We represented family law, landlord/tenant disputes, and poverty law, and we worked with one client at a time. We engaged in what I thought of as Willy-Wonka-golden-ticket law. If someone had no money, or had been turned down by legal aid, they came to us. We listened to everyone who came through our doors or called us on the phone; however, if thirty people a week came to us, we only provided lawyers for one or two. We could make a huge difference to those one or two, and the experience of our staff was very positive during this time because lawyers had the freedom to choose what cases they worked on, with no parameters other than we didn't work in criminal law. In those early days, the Center was a cross between a utopia and the island of misfit lawyers. We didn't have formal job descriptions, but we all found our place. People worked hard for justice and mostly won. But when the dream didn't line up with reality, there was friction.

After my first year there, the board of directors assigned a new direction: don't just be an alternative to legal aid because we already have legal aid in this community; start doing things that legal aid can't or won't do. I agreed with their input because it was a principled direction. We started doing more environmental work and more civil rights cases. We started playing a bigger game and having a bigger impact—not just on the lives of single clients, but on the whole community. We were working to be the voice of the voiceless, and we wanted to find ways to leverage our resources to help even more people than the individuals who visited us.

Staff were on board with the vision, in theory. But to the degree that people had to change their day-to-day activities, some were very opposed. Whereas the work we were doing before had been highly personal and more immediately gratifying, the kind of work the board was suggesting was more abstract. Constitutional and class action issues require more legal rigor and less social work, which means the feel-good encounters with individual clients decreased. As a result, staff weren't feeling as positive about their experiences at work, which dealt a blow to morale and the existing culture of the space. Back when Jim Sheehan was the executive director and funding 100% of operations, people were instructed to "do justice" and were given the autonomy to explore what that meant for themselves and to take on work that aligned with their personal interests and passions. Within the board's new vision, that began to change, and change was hard.

I thought if I was nice enough and a good enough coach, I could take what I knew about management from managing a thirty-person private law firm and use my experience to initiate a shift in culture. I knew that staff—myself included—really valued our opportunity to serve individuals in the community. I decided to initiate this shift with a project that continued the work that people found so meaningful and core to our mission.

We launched a new project called Limited Advocacy, which was a way to bridge the gap between who we were and who we were becoming. We assigned one attorney to oversee a social worker and law student interns. Those students would interview potential clients and figure out what we could do for them short of filing a lawsuit. We addressed the same kinds of issues using a lawyer as supervisor, rather than all of our lawyers engaging with clients directly. We were able to serve more people with a one-quarter-time attorney that year than all the attorneys together were serving the previous year.

Now, we were offering a different level of service. But we were still resolving issues and doing community education. For example, we would explain to people things like: you're crosswise with your landlord right now because you didn't understand the law. When he didn't fix the refrigerator, you should not have stopped paying rent. You have to send your landlord a notice first, and if he doesn't fix it in ten days, then you can stop paying rent. We helped people understand the system, gave them tools for problem solving, and advocated for them with phone calls.

Another benefit of Limited Advocacy was when we wanted to work on bigger issues, we had a list of clients to pull from for class action lawsuits. An example of this was a guy who came to see us whose driver's license had been suspended. The State of Washington suspends 300,000 licenses each year—not for bad driving, but for not paying other tickets. It's basically a war on poverty. Our society is so car-dependent that the system was setting people up to break the law, since it's a crime to drive with a suspended license. What's more, if the authorities in Spokane arrested someone for driving without a license, they also towed the person's car and auctioned it off. You went to jail, and when you got out of jail, your car was gone, and you had a mountain of additional fees you had to pay. It turned out this was unconstitutional according to the Washington State Supreme Court and the United States Supreme Court.

Like many things in Spokane in the early 2000s, the Constitution was sometimes only advisory in practice, and there were few, if any, lawyers doing constitutional law. We took on that case and threatened to sue the City of Spokane. We told them, if you don't resolve this, we will turn it into a class action lawsuit, which means the City would have to go back several years and refund hundreds of thousands of dollars. But we came to an agreement with them that instructed the City to fund a driver's relicensing program for at least three years. They created a pathway for people with suspended licenses to get right with the courts. If you showed a judge you had money for monthly payments, the City would pull tickets out of collection, cut the amount in half (essentially getting rid of some of the interest and penalties), put you on a twenty-five-dollar-a-month payment plan, and give your license back. Then you could legally drive, go to work, support your family, and actually start paying your fines.

The way the system worked before, the City saw millions of dollars in unpaid tickets because you had to pay them all at once or you didn't get your license. No one could do it. If citizens couldn't pay $50 tickets, they definitely couldn't pay an additional $2,000 in interest and penalties. With the payment plans in place, the City started collecting the fees. The money they spent to manage the program was more than paid for by collections. That's the kind of case the CFJ board wanted us to do. The outcome positively impacted the lives of thousands of people. The City stopped repossessing cars, started a relicensing program, and now we didn't have to fight that fight on a case-by-case basis any longer.

Another example of taking the case of a single person in order to

At the front desk of the Center for Justice

improve the quality of life for all was Otto Zehm. This case initiated some of the most widespread changes to our justice system that the City has ever seen. In the early 2000s, citizens were suffering due to a pattern of policing practices that didn't take mental health into account, which resulted in unnecessary violence, trauma, and sometimes death. Otto Zehm's death at the hands of the police, and the case that resulted, changed the cultural perspective of the entire city on police violence. Before that case, everyone assumed that if the police beat up, shot, or killed someone, the victim must have deserved it.

Our case involved Otto Zehm, a janitor with cognitive impairments. On March 18, 2006, Zehm entered a Zip Trip convenience store to purchase a Snickers bar and a bottle of pop. Police officers wrongly identified him as a possible suspect for a reported ATM theft. One officer confronted Zehm, beat him with a baton, and tased him. When six additional officers arrived, they tied him up and continued to forcefully subdue him. He died two days later in the hospital from his injuries.

The City of Spokane and police maintained that any injury suffered by Zehm was brought upon himself due to his aggressive behavior and attempts to resist arrest. But several angles of video footage from the convenience store told a very different story of what happened that night. It showed the officers' aggressions and the victim's attempts to block unprovoked blows to his face and body.

The Center for Justice filed a lawsuit in the U.S. District Court for the Eastern District of Washington on behalf of Otto Zehm and his mother. The first allegation stated that officers violated Otto Zehm's civil rights by: 1) using deadly force upon him when he was only passively resisting an effort to handcuff him, and 2) that deadly force and excessive force were repeatedly used against Mr. Zehm in violation of both his civil rights and the Spokane Police Department's use of force policy. The Spokane County Medical Examiner concluded that the use of force against Mr. Zehm by the officers caused his death.

The second allegation stated that the Spokane Police Department, led by the then acting-chief, engaged in concerted actions to falsely portray Zehm as the initiator of the melee. Our complaint alleged that this conduct was purposeful, and that its purpose was to impede and frustrate the rights of Zehm's mother to be compensated for the violation of her son's rights—a violation which resulted in the death of her son.

Because of cover-ups from the City of Spokane and the police force, the case dragged on until 2011, when one officer was convicted of needlessly beating Zehm and lying to cover up his actions. Other officers were accused of obstruction of justice for their efforts to lie or manipulate the case. Otto Zehm's estate was awarded over $1 million. But more importantly, the City agreed to train all current and future officers in crisis intervention and de-escalation for at least forty hours—a substantial financial investment and cultural shift. Additionally, the police transitioned to a new use-of-force policy, and the public interest in the case set the stage for Spokane's first civilian police ombudsman and other criminal justice reforms.

This kind of case is how the Center for Justice earned public trust. From that point on, the press called the Center to inquire about all kinds of issues. The Center became the conscience and voice of the community on legal issues. And we loved educating the community about those important issues. For this reason, I always took calls from TV stations and the local papers. I tried not to advocate so much for our own case, but rather to present the issue. I'd explain that the other side says this, our client says that, and these are the basic historical principles we are wrestling with. I tried to help people in the community get underneath the rhetoric and draw their own conclusions. This consistent open communication with public channels is one of the ways we approached a city with Midwestern sensibilities and showed the public a more inclusive understanding of justice. If you wanted to know about legal justice in Spokane, the Center for Justice was the first stop.

We were able to earn this influence, in part, thanks to Jim's support for the Center. Our private funding meant we could act nimbly and pursue important cases, even if they wouldn't make money. No law firm in the city would have touched Otto Zehm's case because of how much attorney time, and therefore up-front costs, it required. Nor would any traditional law firm have wanted to take on two of the most embedded power structures in a community: the City and the police. But thanks to Jim's open-ended call to "do justice" and his full financial support of the hard work it took to follow that call, the Center truly became a voice for the voiceless and helped make Spokane a city where more people experienced justice.

Another clear example of this is Smart Justice Spokane, a broad coalition of over thirty organizations working together to end mass incarceration and eliminate racial disparities in our local criminal justice system. Coalition partners believe that the recovery and integration of those caught up in the criminal justice system is essential for a strong, healthy, and just community. Smart Justice was conceived of at a retreat for Community Building organizations. I remember breaking out for lunch and eating with the directors of Greater Spokane Progress, the Peace and Justice Action League, and the Community Building Foundation. Conversation turned to the upcoming ballot proposal to build a new jail in Spokane County. We knew that the initiative would likely be voted down due to the ongoing recession, but the economy would bounce back. We needed to get ahead of this issue. Initially, we called the campaign No New Jails, but it soon transformed into Smart Justice—a call for evidence-based and effective practices for criminal justice reform.

At our first symposium in 2013, we invited local businesses, prosecutors, police, sheriffs, county commissioners, the mayor, and city council. I was no longer at the Center, but I stayed involved and continued as the chairperson of Smart Justice. Experts from across the nation presented about criminal justice reform in their own communities. We knew it would be hard to get those stakeholders together again, so we packed the day with way more content than you normally would. The most memorable part included a real-time dial where everyone in the room could "agree" or "disagree" with live questions. We discovered that when people were in their "talking heads" role, they tended to voice conservative opinions. But in real time, when asked questions anonymously, the majority disagreed with the elected sheriff and mayor. Publicly, everyone stayed in their own silos, but they could anonymously dial their indicator and express their true beliefs. That day changed the world in Spokane, since people in "The System" recognized that they shared values and could work together on this issue to actually change things.

I am incredibly proud of the Center for Justice and all the ways we helped make the City of Spokane a more just place for all. The charge from the board to strive to be a bigger player in the community was a huge part of that. But there was another big change that made my job even more challenging and came close to pulling the Center apart. When Jim hired me, he said, "Breean, one thing you'll never have to do is any fundraising." That gave me permission to focus 100% of my time and attention on all the ways we could pursue justice. It was a dream come true for any nonprofit leader to not have to compete for resources, and instead grow the mission and impact of the organization.

But two years after I arrived, Jim decided, or perhaps it had been on his mind all along, that the Center for Justice should be the people's law firm. He wanted us to transition from an angel-funded project with absolute autonomy and freedom to a donor-based model.

This was a challenging proposition for many reasons. First, within eighteen months of initiating this change, the stock market crashed, and funding opportunities dried up all over the place. Secondly, I wasn't the right director for that job; I did not have the skill set for, or experience in, fundraising. Third, our attorneys didn't want to do it. Staff had been operating under the same impression I had been, and the security they felt knowing their jobs weren't fundraiser-dependent seemed to be in jeopardy for the first time.

Finally, funding legal aid is very low on the list of areas that private donors typically fund. They will fund food and shelter and children, but legal services are a much harder sell. The impact is simply not perceived as clearly or as immediately. When you feed someone and shelter someone, you can relate as a human being to that experience, and you're putting food on their table, now. Legal services have huge impacts on individuals and entire communities, but it's not immediate gratification. The legal system works slowly, for one thing. And for another, structural forces want things to remain the way they are. For example, some people who profit off the existing system likely don't want landlords who abuse tenants to be held accountable. They don't want employers who face discrimination charges to be held liable. They actively resist accountability and put out messaging that makes it harder to fundraise.

Ironically, what made fundraising challenging was also inherent to the organization's structure and the source of its power: we were able to work on the most significant cases, regardless of how much they would cost. This made us a serious threat to the existing power structures and gave us the autonomy to be real players in the community. Very few organizations have this kind of clout because they are forced to live within their grant- and donor-directed missions, and most donors aren't keen on financing this kind of time-consuming, policy-changing, high-impact litigation. However, when we tried to raise money, donors said, "Jim's got plenty of money, and it's his baby." Even when we finally got a good development director in place, the change was too abrupt.

I do think it would have been easier to transition to a donor-based organization if Jim had known to be clearer about this intention from the beginning, and I had asked tougher questions. It is an unusual proposition to fund and fully sustain a nonprofit for seven years, then transition its funding base in such a radical way. But those early years did allow the Center to find its identity and establish public trust. The Center also added some new and important environmental programs to its docket prior to the economic downturn. Based on what I know now, I should have argued that we should not add new programs until we had a more fleshed-out financial plan for Jim's transition to a community-funded law firm. And I should have addressed the staff conflict with the Board's new mission more directly, rather than hoping it would work out over time with me simply serving as a mediator.

Jim wanted to get to a place where the community owned the law firm, but at decision points he injected cash into the system rather than scale back or make hard decisions. He never wanted to fire anyone. He never wanted good programs to go away. And as a non-confrontational person, he never addressed the hard changes that would need to be made to transition to donor support. He had hired everyone there personally and he was incredibly loyal. I shared some of the same impulses as Jim and was hopeful that we would turn the corner despite the Great Recession. Ultimately, it was a heavy lift for both of us and exhausting to navigate.

I transitioned from my work at the Center in 2010 and took my public service in a different direction. I served on city council for four years and am now city council president. I can confidently say that, even though the Center sunset as an organization in 2020, it has permanently and positively changed the cultural fabric of Spokane. Because of the Center, ideas like protecting the river, community-oriented policing, and Smart Justice are integrated into the values of our city. There are now enough people championing those causes that the Spokane community can pick up where the Center left off.

There were all kinds of decision points along the way that we could have

Breean Beggs, the Center of Justice's first executive director

done differently if we had known the future. One thing is for sure: the concept is a winner. It just needs to be scaled to financial resources available within the community, whether it's from one family or a whole group of supporters. Part of the problem was that all of our hearts were a little too big, and our vision too broad. We thought, surely, we're doing such good work that this will eventually be financially sustainable. But it takes more than that. You have to have the optimism and the faith, and you have to have a scalable financial plan.

That said, the same issues that I was passionate about at the Center, and that we worked so hard on while I was there—police reform, criminal justice reform, and the health of the Spokane River—that work continues. We are not going backwards. We're actually blossoming and getting the benefit of all that work finally coming to fruition.

I can see clearly from my vantage point as city council president that all the work that we accomplished through the Center created a foundation for a lot of the work we're doing today. For example, I'm the only person on city council who was engaged in river issues back in the mid-2000s. When we're having debates about what to do next to clean up the river, no one remembers that the community was at war with the City and the County over pollution standards. All the basic protections for the river in terms of river flow and pollution control, those are all in place, and we are striving to make a river that is even cleaner and more accessible to more everyday people. The City is opening the cleanest sewage plant that's ever existed on the Spokane River. And we now spend hundreds of millions of taxpayer funds to ensure the river cleanliness for the next generations. The demand for a cleaner river is not an issue anymore because we won the hearts and minds of people. Without the Center for Justice and Jim's specific funding for a river attorney, that would not have happened.

When I turn to police reform, we are now in a post-George-Floyd world. But Spokane is ahead of most mid-sized cities on police reform because of the work the Center started on policing issues. Now, every patrol officer has forty hours of crisis intervention training. We're doing community policing; we have youth initiatives; we have independent civil oversight and a police ombudsman; and we accomplished forty-two police reforms that the Obama-era Department of Justice recommended. All those things are a given now. Moving forward, we will convene a whole new conversation on police reform to be even more responsive to the community. In the next year, I anticipate we will leap ahead—not just of other cities our size, but of bigger cities, thanks to that head start. The Center closing its doors doesn't diminish that. In fact, the ongoing impacts of the Center's work shows that the Board's decision to focus on impact litigation and on reforms that changed policy and institutional practice was a visionary decision. Now, that resource allocation is paying dividends.

It's important to remember that the struggle to create more justice—whether it's environmental justice, racial justice, social justice, or economic justice—is ongoing. It will never end. Our human condition means the struggle is ongoing. There will be higher and higher bars of morality and standards of justice that we will be called to meet and exceed—and, as we succeed, the bar will get even higher.

So, the question is always for each individual, what is he or she going to do personally, as part of the struggle? And the question for the community is, what kind of institutions do we support? Are we going to support justice-creating institutions that do really hard and sometimes thankless work, particularly on behalf of those who have no voice or power? Are we going to financially invest in the moral arc that Martin Luther King Jr. talked about, the one that's long and bends towards justice? I think that during the twenty years that its doors were open, the Center for Justice and its employees filled both roles so wonderfully. It set an example for all individuals to follow through on their particular call to create justice. And it gave the community an institution whose legacy continues to inspire more opportunities for all people to experience justice.

CHAPTER EIGHT

Child Care as Social Justice

By Anita Morgan

Anita was the executive director of Blueprints for Learning from 2004 to 2019 and director of the Community Building Children's Center from 2004 to 2020. She helped improve the quality of child care across the region by providing focused educational and support services to the greater Spokane community of child care providers.

Every working parent has to face the challenge of finding quality child care, and everyone dreams of having their beloved children in an ideal situation. Regrettably, it's a pipe dream for many families because it's not available or it's not affordable. Jim Sheehan decided he would make it available by recruiting child care professionals to launch the Community Building Children's Center (CBCC), and he would make it affordable by subsidizing it. He went a step further when he made it sustainable by supporting the development of the Child Care Training Institute (CCTI). The teachers that graduate from the institute's various offerings go on to become practitioners and advocates for quality child care and early childhood education.

I became involved with the Community Building Campus when my friend and colleague, Lynne Sanders, approached me about joining the effort to elevate child care and early childhood education through the programs at Blueprints for

Learning. How could we put together a viable, sustainable child care program from scratch? First, we needed a guiding philosophy. Lynne and I had been early childhood educators and advocates for years and knew what we wanted, but we also knew the obstacles. There is a lot of talk about the importance of early childhood education, but it has traditionally been undervalued, and as a result, underfunded. One world-renowned exception can be found in the city of Reggio Emilia in northern Italy. The Community Building Children's Center is a school that uses the wider urban environment as its classroom and is inspired by the Reggio Emilia model.

The Campus as Classroom

The big windows facing Main Avenue give the children a bird's-eye of the sidewalk and its denizens, and everyone who passes by gets a glimpse into the everyday lives of children. The children can see if it's rainy, snowy, or sunny. A passerby will see them sitting at wood tables in wood chairs, doing art projects or having a snack. They might even see kids with a parent or grandparent, enjoying a snack or reading together in the cozy rocking chair. The warren of rooms at the interior of the center provides spaces for quiet play, nap time, and more focused learning activities.

Children enter the Community Building lobby through a set of old, full-light, golden oak swinging doors repurposed from the original building. The street-level lobby opens up to high ceilings and the upper floor of the mezzanine with its signature bulbous sculpture and Kizuri fair trade shop with its colors, textures, and scents. On the ground level there is a scattering of comfy couches and chairs oriented to a faux fireplace front and an upright piano anyone can play. There are people coming and going—people the children recognize, and people they have never seen before. Imagine what it's like for these young children to have this rich and dynamic area to pass through multiple times every day!

The Children's Center incorporates the breadth of the building's ground floor, including an outdoor play area that faces the alley where there is a mix of activity—not all of it pretty. This exposure was considered and planned for. Kids are secure behind a beautifully designed, wrought iron fence, and there is a vegetated buffer. Investment in the feel of the play area is obvious in other ways, too. Due to the space restrictions of an urban campus, the play yard has two

Children play with a teacher inside the Children's Center

levels, with a natural water feature bubbling from upright rocks that spill into a small rocky creek, trees, and shrubs. Nooks and crannies provide small, child-scale spaces, and flexible pieces of equipment that promote big body play—as well as imaginative play—are placed throughout the play yard.

Quality materials enhance quality play, and Jim is committed to both throughout the building to enhance the lives of children and adults. The idea is that if you invest in good stuff up front, you will have lower maintenance and replacement costs in the long run. So, less plastic and more durable natural materials like wood. Interestingly, lots of ideal materials aren't expensive at all. Water, sand, mud, and big cardboard appliance boxes inspire hours of engaged, inventive, and meaningful play for children.

It's wonderful to be able to access so many different spaces around the campus, and for the children to experience an urban program with an environment rich for learning. The toddlers frequent the Community Building lobby, where they have a secret cabinet full of toys and little bikes to scoot around on. For a long time, we gardened a rooftop space in the Community Building. Along with their teachers, Warrin Bazille (Chapter 6) helped children plant vegetables in the classroom and then transfer them to the big planter boxes on the Community Building rooftop. Throughout the growing season, small groups of children visited the rooftop garden several times a week for observing, marveling, watering, weeding, and eventually harvesting their tiny crops of green beans, tomatoes, strawberries, and snap peas. We also partnered with the Main Market Co-op by having the children start plants from seed that then graduate to the Co-op greenhouse. The children have even cultivated enough plants to have a plant sale, which thrilled them to no end.

Visiting various parts of the campus is often the highlight of our day. We like going to visit parents that work in the buildings. Sometimes we load everyone up into the bye-bye buggy and stroll around. We love that we have a beautiful campus that allows us to explore, enjoy green spaces, and wander close to the Spokane River. One year, our children were extra-enamored with pretending to make and serve coffee and tea. In small groups, we walked down to Café Affogato, located in the Saranac Commons, to have the barista give them a tour behind the counter and show them the steps in making a cup of espresso. Getting a close-up look at this process captivated the children's interest and attention. The children were able to help choose from the selection of tea and treats and enjoy a mid-morning tea break at the cafe. Later, back at school, the experience showed up with more detailed, complex play about preparing and serving coffee and tea. We have partnered with the Magic Lantern movie theater to show a children's movie for a special experience on pajama day, premiere a preschool-class-produced stop-motion animation of the sinking of the Titanic, and show a family movie as a fundraiser. This has helped introduce the theater to a broader audience and raised the visibility of our programs.

It's so important and meaningful for families to have on-site child care beyond the convenience and time savings. Proximity absolutely makes a big difference, especially when the children are really young. It's much easier for nursing mothers to come down in the middle of the day if they are in the building than if they have to drive across town. They don't have to pump or take as much time away from work, and they get to integrate their relationship with their child into the workday. Fathers can also feed and bond with their little ones. Parents and grandparents are often special guests at lunch, birthday celebrations, and other special occasions.

At CBCC, parents can also plug into a bigger vision. Parents have often told me that this place is in alignment with their aspirations, values, and the kind of world they hope to create for their children and their families. Being in the Community Building Annex has been good for me, our teachers, parents, and children because we're constantly running into other people. This is especially important considering that many child care centers are in people's homes or their own buildings, which isolates them. Children, their teachers, and their families all deserve an enriched and relationship-based environment. They deserve a loving and nurturing opportunity to be a part of a healthy community.

It was also good for me personally to be in a building with many other organizations. I was busy fundraising and growing our programs, but I loved knowing what was going on in other organizations and likely wouldn't have time to seek that out if I weren't in that space every day. I retired in early 2020, and now that I have more time to pursue something other than my own work, I know right where to plug in!

The Reggio Emilia Model in Spokane

The citizens of Reggio Emilia demonstrated their dedication to young children starting soon after the end of World War II. Community members support children and families by investing in consistent funding for their care and enrichment. Part of the city budget—somewhere between 12 to 14%—is allocated annually for a system of high-quality municipal infant/toddler centers and preschools. Families still pay some tuition, but they could never afford such high-quality care without dedicated and reliable funding through the city.

We don't have the City of Spokane subsidizing child care like Reggio Emilia does, but we do have Jim. Since the very earliest stages of CBCC's development, his support has given us the great gift of being able to dream big. Once we agreed to Reggio Emilia as the guiding philosophy for the Children's Center, we were able to design a physical space that fit with our vision of a model environment for children. It was enormously liberating not to have to follow an institutional-type model. While many of our services are fee-based, we also rely on grants, sponsors, and our annual fundraiser, the Great Spokane Art Party, to support our efforts to improve child care, early learning, and child care teacher training and mentoring for the greater Spokane area.

In the U.S., we are so deep in the survival-mode mentality when it comes to child care that it's been nearly impossible to lift our heads up high enough to imagine what else is possible for our children: a model of quality where children play happily and interact in environments rich in beautiful and interesting materials; guided by engaged, educated, thoughtful teachers who receive the professional support they need to excel at their profession; families that partner

Photo by Rajah Bose

The Children's Center's urban outdoor playground

with us and benefit from their child's emotional, social, and intellectual well-being and their own sense of peace of mind and support for being the kind of parents they want to be. In Spokane, Jim's commitment to easing some of the attendant financial burdens has allowed us to not only dream big, but to realize our dream.

Reggio Emilia has shared with the world an image of children that is respectful and shows children, families, and communities what powerful thinkers and learners they are. Reggio's groundbreaking work was asking teachers to slow down and see themselves as co-learners. This invigorates teachers to participate in the full unfolding of a child's development. The Reggio philosophy equips teachers to be respectful and observant and to meet children where they are—not as blank slates, but "as beautiful, powerful, competent, creative, curious, and full of potential and ambitious desires," as described by early childhood education scholar Valarie Hewitt.

In addition to prioritizing relationships with fellow students and teachers, Reggio focuses on children as active hands-on learners, curious and inquisitive. They engage with a rich variety of multi-sensory materials such as shells, seed pods, fabrics, building blocks, paints, pencils, markers, and recycled castoffs that are thoughtfully arranged in the learning environment by the teachers.

Through manipulating and interacting directly with these materials, and in interactions with their peers and teachers, children build their understanding of how the world works; they literally construct their knowledge as they play. The Reggio-inspired approach makes this learning visible through written and visual documentation of children and teachers at work. We do this work at CBCC on a regular basis through daily journals we send home to families and through our annual exhibit, *The Creativity of Children.*

The daily journals are written by lead teachers and serve as windows into the classroom for parents. They also help make learning visible to teachers and help them reflect on their teaching practices. This reflective process is a continual professional development tool for teachers, and it invites parents to more deeply participate in a child's learning. This is especially important for parents who are not a daily part of the campus, such as community member Ellen Welcker with two children who have attended the Community Building Children's Center. Ellen writes:

The daily journals that are an integral part of CBCC's documentation are sent home at the end of the day, usually just before pickup time. These journals are a quick read—they offer us a glimpse into the day's work, which often includes group problem-solving, engaging with wonder, artistic exploration, and coming together to celebrate milestones in the children's lives. They give us, as parents and caretakers, the gift of a touchstone on which to start conversations with our children, without having to resort to the dead-end: "What happened at school today?" In our family, they have helped us to use consistent language and messaging between home and school with regard to resolving conflict. They model for us ways to structure or re-conceive our play with our own children—for example, the incredible intention with which the teachers ask questions of themselves and their work with the kids. Consider this excerpt of a few weeks ago, in the toddler room:

"The CBCC toddlers have continued to be enthusiastic about our long-term worm investigation. After thinking more about the toddlers' interactions with, and representations of, the worms, we decided to modify our original hypothesis: The toddlers' fascination with bugs comes from the bugs' size, fragility, and their unpredictable movements. Our new hypothesis is: The toddlers' interest in and behavior with the worms is directed toward forming connections with these other creatures that are part of the natural world. This week I noticed several games and strategies our toddlers used with one another, and with the worms, to create bonds and friendships."

The journal goes on to illustrate the myriad ways in which the children interact with the worms, and yes, there are incredibly cute pictures.

And in the preschool room, where several children have recently become older siblings, play recently has turned to reenacting the birth of a baby:

"I wondered what questions were being answered for them and what questions were being created around birth. Going to the hospital was important to both their experiences, but how do shots and medicine fit in? For pain? Because you need them? They both spoke about what happens afterwards, taking pictures together and handling the baby gently."

This entry goes on to affirm that the play holds deep meaning in gaining understanding surrounding a birth in the family—physically, emotionally, and culturally.

The daily journals are just one of many accessible paths to communicate with our children and their teachers at CBCC, but I'm so grateful to the staff for their dedication to this mindful practice, and for sharing them with us for the benefit of all.

This social-emotional component has proven to be critical, as socially and emotionally skilled children begin formal school with a sense of security and confidence. When adults are interested in children, when children have interactions that support feelings of acceptance, they feel secure. Language development and critical thinking are also influenced by child-adult interactions. These interactions are facilitated when schools have adequate structural features in place, which includes low student-to-teacher ratios, a living wage for teachers, and professional development opportunities so teachers can continue to learn and grow. These structural components lead to increased teacher retention, which means young professionals have the chance to become skilled teachers rather than part of the two-to-three-year revolving door the industry is known for.

Solutions for Systemic Challenges

This revolving door also contributes to more systemic challenges in education. Disparities in education develop even before children begin formal schooling and is why we believe that child care is an important social justice issue. You may have heard of the "million-word gap" as a way to talk about the disparity in quality in children's early learning. A 2019 study out of Ohio State University found that young children whose parents or caregivers read them five

Anita Morgan has improved child care both at the CBCC and across the region

books a day entered kindergarten with crucial building blocks for success, having heard 1.4 million more words than kids who were never read to. Children of working parents might spend up to ten hours a day in group care, and their families can only hope that their care providers are equipped for the task.

This is why we did not stop with launching our own child care center and we began to daydream about the Child Care Training Institute (CCTI). My co-educator and the founder of Blueprints for Learning, Lynne, was diagnosed with terminal cancer in 2003, the year after she founded the Community Building Children's Center. This added even more urgency to the project and made me want to follow through with our common vision. In addition to a child care center, Lynne wanted to make sure she could continue to do advocacy and adult education as well, so we brought over a program we had been working on for several years through the Spokane Regional Health District, the Child Development Associate (CDA) + Mentoring Training Program. This successful program became the flagship of the training institute. Each year we supported a cohort of twenty to twenty-five teachers already working in local child care programs in a one-night-a-week, twelve-month program. To help teachers put into place what they learned in class, their CDA instructor/mentor would do site visits and provide feedback while visiting each teacher's child care classroom.

The CDA + Mentoring was a very accessible program that helped a lot of teachers see themselves as capable professionals and inspired interest in continuing their education at the AA and BA levels. The cohort model built in time for peer interaction and peer support. This program was also the primary vehicle through which we fulfilled our larger mission of improving the quality of early care and education in the Spokane area. We worked with roughly three hundred and fifty teachers through Blueprints for Learning to earn their CDA credential. The program ran continuously for twenty years, until 2018, when a change in state regulations made the program impossible to run. We are no longer able to offer the CDA + Mentoring Program. CCTI still exists but is much scaled down. However, the new leadership and board are continuing to move the vision for this part of our organization forward.

We have a guiding philosophy and a beautiful space. Jim's contribution, in the form of a rent subsidy, provides financial stability and security and makes the school more affordable for everyone. Our rent subsidy also enables us to have better teacher-child ratios than the state requires. It allows us to more easily pay, train, and retain teachers, which is crucial for childhood development. Children need stable relationships, which is hard to provide given the revolving door of early childhood education teachers. It also allows us to accept some families that qualify for state subsidies because state funds only cover a percentage of the total cost.

Jim's support also allows us to give teachers planning and curriculum development time during the day and to take six professional development days across the year. Teachers have both a one-hour curriculum reflection and development meeting and a one-hour team planning meeting weekly. This is considered best practice in the field but is seldom available to teachers in early-care settings. It costs money because we must have the extra staff to sub in the classrooms while the teachers are in these meetings. Professional development days are full days devoted to teacher training and development. The teachers attend a full day of professional development without children in attendance, and we have early closure days the other six months during the year for staff meetings. These days are scheduled annually and given to families on an annual calendar so they can plan alternate care for these days. I remember when I first considered including this component as part of our program and was concerned that I might have a riot on my hands. But parents were accepting, despite the inconvenience to their schedules. Thankfully, parents can see that well-valued, professionally supported, and compensated teachers return an enhanced level of investment and engagement for the children they care for and educate.

Both CBCC and CCTI show that early childhood education is an integral part of a more holistic vision for how to nourish social change. We are building healthy human capacity and leveling the social, emotional, and intellectual playing field for children in our community. We see children as current citizens, not future citizens, and believe they have the capacity to contribute now. We understand that the ability to develop higher-order thinking and healthy social emotional skills can begin very early and have a lifelong impact.

CHAPTER NINE

Thin Air Community Radio

By Shahrokh Nikfar

Shahrokh is an assistant director at the Northwest Fair Housing Alliance, where he has worked for eighteen years. His show The Persian Hour *was one of the first and longest-running shows at KYRS. He was also the founder of Caffe Affogato and Mediterrano in the Saranac Commons building.*

You are probably familiar with National Public Radio and its many signature programs. NPR is a full-power public station, akin in its reach to the thousands of commercial radio stations around the country. You may not be familiar, though, with a more intimate and local brand of public radio station—low-power, non-commercial, FM radio—dubbed LPFM community stations. This type of station was first opened up by the Federal Communications Commission in 1999 in response to public demand for more public stations.

Most LPFM stations were relegated to small towns since the FM band was full in large urban areas. But, lucky for me, Spokane was a rare case where a larger metro area had one open frequency. I say lucky for me because Spokane's low-power radio station, KYRS Thin Air Radio, has changed my life.

Photo by Jon Snyder

Shahrokh Nikfar, host of KYRS's *The Persian Hour*

I came to the U.S. by myself as a sixteen-year-old student on November 21, 1978 to finish my senior year in a high school in Texas. Soon after I arrived, there was political upheaval in Iran and a group of student radicals took some American embassy staff hostage and held them for four hundred and forty-four days. During my first year, the kids at my new high school talked with me, and the girls thought I was cute. But soon after the hostage crisis started, I was seen and treated as an enemy of the state.

I endured physical, mental, and emotional abuse every single day. Nobody protected me, not even the teachers. Throughout the upcoming years of my life in America, I felt unwelcome and discriminated against. Then I got my job at Northwest Fair Housing Alliance (NWFHA) in Spokane in 2003 and started coming regularly to the Community Building. It took a while for me to understand the concept of this environment, as it was all new and refreshing to me. Prior to working at NWFHA, I had worked for several corporations, and the CBC environment was completely different from the corporate culture I was used to. Gradually, I began to feel safe for the first time since I had come to America. Not only did I feel accepted and celebrated, but I also began to feel empowered by the community's embrace.

One of the many inspiring people I met while working at the Community Building was Lupito Flores, a guy who enjoyed laughing with me when I shared stories about my childhood in Iran. Lupito is the founding manager of Spokane's Thin Air Community Radio station, an endeavor he co-created with other activists. The station first went on the air from the third floor of the Community Building Annex in 2003, and shortly thereafter, Lupito invited me to come on the air and tell some of my stories. We decided to turn my one-off stories into a show because I wanted to expose Spokanites to a version of Iran and Iranians they had no opportunity to see or hear about.

The mainstream media's bias and agenda has often focused on demonizing Iranians and anyone from the Middle East or Western Asia. At times, this fear has been used to justify atrocities against other human beings. I felt a calling to undo some of this harm and to humanize my homeland by sharing my own personal experiences through stories of my childhood in Iran, travels to Iran, and interviews with people who had some real knowledge of Iran—and mix it all with recipes and music. I wanted to make a difference for the better—no matter how small—and I wanted to have some fun along the way. So, I started my show, and called it *The Persian Hour*.

The tensions between the U.S. and Iran were still high, and I remember talking on one of my early shows about a question put to Senator John McCain by a constituent: "It's well documented that we have, for quite a long time now, known where the real problem is in the Middle East. . . . When do we send them an air mail message to Tehran?" McCain responded with a remake of the old Beach Boys song to the tune of "Barbara Anne," singing, "Bomb Bomb Bomb, Bomb Bomb Iran." Everyone in that audience laughed as I imagined my loved ones being torn into pieces of burning flesh by American bombs.

This was just one of thousands of examples of how Iran and Iranians were and still are referred to by politicians and the media. When I watch movies and TV shows or listen to the news on the radio about the Middle East, I detect all the fearmongering and manipulation masked as patriotism. The mainstream media was relentless in creating fear and justifying horrific acts of violence against other humans. Gradually, I began adding some short commentaries about what I was seeing and how the rhetoric was affecting me. I didn't want to preach at the listeners or judge or blame them; I just wanted to be honest and share what my heart wanted to say. The music, stories, and humor made the message more palatable for listeners. One of the stories I told about growing up in Iran is my chicken story.

Photo by Rajah Bose

Inside the studio at KYRS

I attended grade school in Tehran, a beautiful cosmopolitan city with similarities to the old parts of Paris and the new parts of modern New York. My twenty-five-minute walk to and from grade school was a fragrant journey through narrow streets where kitchen windows were opened for ventilation and released the aromas of saffron, garlic, mint, fried potatoes, and eggplants simmering in a tomato sauce. I passed bakeries with fresh bread being pulled out of ovens, vegetable stands and butcher shops, bookstores, tea stores, coffee houses, and the occasional fortune teller or musician playing an instrument for a few coins.

One morning on the way to school, when I was about seven years old, I saw a young white chicken running through the busy street, trying to survive oncoming traffic. I didn't know where he had come from, but I ran in the middle of the traffic to save him. I caught it and desperately wanted to take the chicken home with me, but I was going to be late to school. So, I knocked on a nearby door to a stranger's house. A woman in her thirties wearing a yellow dress with prints of flowers answered, and I asked her to look after my chicken. Hours later, I showed up promptly after school to retrieve my friend.

When I arrived home from school, I told my mom the story and let her know the chicken was my new pet. The only place for the chicken to reside was the garden. Every house in Iran has a Persian garden, which inspired the historic Spanish gardens with fruit and flowing water. Our courtyard had meandering pathways and a table and chairs positioned next to a small fountain, shaded by fruit trees, and surrounded by roses. A majority of these types of houses have now been replaced by modern high-rise apartments to accommodate a 600% surge in population. But these high rises are required to have small parks in their building plans that imitate Persian gardens. Our garden was the place where my parents enjoyed the pleasant evening breeze with a cup of tea and relaxed at the end of the day, while my pet ran around and pooped everywhere and grew into a beautiful, plump, white chicken.

One day I got home from school, and my chicken wasn't anywhere to be seen. I looked for him nervously and then asked my mom about him. She told me he needed to go and get married and create a family, and he had said goodbye before he left.

That night my mom made an amazing chicken dish with saffron, red berries called zeresk, orange zest, slivers of almonds, pistachios, and other spices. She then prepared a plate for one of our neighbors and asked me to deliver it. As I walked over carrying the aromatic plate of food, I noticed that the chicken leg on the plate was larger than the normal chicken legs she bought from the store. It was the best chicken I've ever had.

When I told this story on my radio show, I followed it with the statement: And now I have a chicken recipe for you! I also told this story when I helped with fundraising. I took the fundraising challenge seriously, and my show was always in the top three for raising money. Since there was no Persian restaurant in Spokane, twice a year during our fund drive I raffled a seven- to ten-course meal on air. The phone rang off the hook. We usually raised between $1,000 to $2,000 over that hour. Sometimes I would go to the winner's house, and sometimes they would come to mine. I made halume, a Greek cheese that you fry and douse in lemon juice. It's salty and delicious, and it excites your taste buds. I often served a special Shirazi salad, from the same region as the wine. The rice dishes in Iran are aromatic, colorful, and beautiful to look at, with saffron, herbs, meat, and rice in between each layer. After a few other dishes, I finished with dozens of pieces of baklava and Turkish coffee and read the grounds, telling everyone's fortunes.

Every show host assisted with fundraising, and funding was always the station's biggest challenge. Community radio is community-run in every sense— and has been since the very beginning. Spokane's Thin Air station was just a dream in 1999, and it took four years to launch the first broadcast. First, there was the matter of obtaining an FCC permit with its strict requirements—100 watts or less, non-profit, and non-commercial. The station had to be four clicks away from another station on both sides of the dial, and if a commercial station upgraded its power, a nearby low-power station would have to go dark or power down so as not to interfere with the commercial station. These low-power stations were considered "secondary service," doubtless a concession to commercial radio interests. It took two full years and a lot of work to receive a permit to broadcast from the FCC. After that, it took eight months to build the physical station. This involved locating and preparing the tower site, erecting the 120-foot tower with partially donated local union labor, wiring the studio (in the Community Building Annex) and transmitter sites, filing permits, and paying fees.

Another aspect of building the station included soliciting a vision for the station and program proposals from Spokane residents. The group of co-founders—among them long-time community activist Rusty Nelson—decided that Thin Air Radio's goal would be to build a strong, listener-supported, community radio station that empowers people—especially ethnic minorities, low-income, and other marginalized groups—to strive for a more just and sustainable world. Their first day of broadcasting was October 26, 2003, from the Community Building Annex, with a dozen live programs hosted by volunteers from the community. Jim Sheehan had actively recruited Lupito and other volunteers to house the station at the Community Building Campus because he believed in the project of public radio and wanted to invest in non-commercial news coverage and programming.

The CBC provided a pool for show hosts, and Lupito worked hard to recruit diverse programming filled with heart, passion, and intelligence since he was surrounded by interdisciplinary people: social justice volunteers and activists, musicians and artists, politicians and professionals. When these show hosts entered the KYRS soundproof studio, sat behind the microphone, and slid their fingers over the sound desk, I believe they felt supported and connected because the radio station is not a separate entity. Rather, it's a limb of a whole body that makes the Community Building.

One of the longest-running shows is *Earth Matters Now*, co-hosted by Mike Peterson and Laura Ackerman, who were long-time employees from the Lands Council. Sam Mace of Save Our Wild Salmon, another organization in the CBC, has been on programs over the years. People from the Center for Justice came on a lot and talked about river and environmental issues that don't get much mainstream media attention. A lot of the police accountability awareness in the city has come from our interviews and news. For example, KYRS interviewed Breean Beggs and broke the Otto Zehm story that initiated police reforms across the city (Chapter 7)

While KYRS was a low-power station, we leased tower space for free on Denise Attwood's property (Chapter 11). This allowed us to grow that station before taking on additional costs. Now we pay $9,000 a year to lease a mountain top tower 40 miles north of Spokane from the Department of Natural Resources. This tower rent is one of our biggest expenses. The station operated as an LPFM until 2011 when we did another capital campaign to raise money to become a full-power station. We now operate at 6800 watts, which is still tiny compared to commercial stations and public radio. Our current class is non-commercial educational. Public radio is in a different class and is more focused on running national programming. Our translator tower three miles north of downtown Spokane costs $350 a month just to power the transmitter. Most of the lower-power FM stations are located in rural areas, so communities can install a small tower near town and an antenna on their roof. Because we need much more power to broadcast to an urban area, our antenna has to be on a mountain top. It takes two hours to drive to the mountaintop, and in winter it is sometimes impassable.

According to Lupito, a few years ago the station went dark, and we had to pay a guy who owned a snowcat to take our volunteer engineer up the mountain during a snowstorm. The snowcat driver could only go at night. He had large spotlights mounted on the front of his snowcat, but whiteout conditions meant he couldn't see the forest service road. At one point he stopped and tried to step off the cat to peer into the darkness and get a sense of his surroundings. He plunged into the snow up to his chin and had to struggle to grasp the cat and pull himself back up. His partner looked off the other side, and they were within a few feet of the edge of the cliff. A large commercial station has a full-time engineer on staff. If anything goes wrong, it's that person's job to work on it. Our guy has a full-time day job and serves the community as he can during his free time.

The move to full power has made a huge difference, and I remember Lupito working very hard toward it. Before, our reach was very limited, and the sound quality wasn't that good. Back then, one of my friends, who lived in downtown Spokane, would sit in her car with a blanket and thermos of coffee to listen to

Photo by Jon Snyder

Nikfar has introduced many Spokanites to new Middle Eastern perspectives and causes

the show because she couldn't get the station inside her apartment and her car acted as an antenna. When we went full power, she could listen inside. Around this time, I started getting calls from people farther away and in more rural areas like Newport, Washington. A guy who called himself Hillbilly Dave called to say he lived in the mountains and listened to my show every weekend. This is an audience I always wanted to reach, and I was so happy to hear from him.

Doing my show every Saturday for so many years was sometimes difficult and took a lot of energy, research, and creativity, so I would start thinking of ending my show. But these emails, letters, and phone calls from random listeners telling me how much they had enjoyed what I shared was enough to refuel me and get going again. More and more, I came across random people who recognized me and energized me with their love and support. Three different times, I was recognized at grocery stores and a coffee shop by the sound of my voice and greeted with smiles and appreciation.

KYRS is unique and based on the character and experiences of every host, every volunteer, and every listener. We were all trying to make the world a little better through our creativity and our sharing. That's what I grew to love about this radio station. There's no corporate policy or agenda that we have to push. Everyone is free to express themselves. There is much beauty at the soul of the station because so many of us cared and were passionate about the things we wanted to share. For example, *Queer Sounds* is the only local program that plays music and host interviews with primarily lesbian, gay, bisexual, transgender, and queer artists. *Queer Sounds* is a very different show than *The Persian Hour*, but both are about the opportunity to say: Here we are, we exist, we are happy people, we love to dance, we love to laugh, and we have beautiful lives. What a rewarding experience for everyone to be able to have the freedom to express themselves publicly, celebrate themselves, and share that celebration with the public.

I was at the station for so long that I was able to help inspire new show hosts. To train them, I would bring them on my show as a guest or a co-host. For a while, there was a show called the *Russian Hour* by a Jewish Russian friend of mine. Later, I trained a Palestinian American friend to do a show. She adopted my approach, as did a show called *Humaculture* about African American culture. I feel that our approach has created awareness, understanding, peace, and love. Nelson Mandela believed that you can't hate people if you know their stories. That's a concept we all used on our shows.

Being a radio host has opened many doors over the years. Back in 2008, I was watching a BBC interview of a young Iranian couple who sold everything they had, bought a couple of bicycles, and rode their bikes around the world planting peace trees. Their names were Jafar and Nasim Edirisi, and I emailed them and said, if you come to the U.S., please come to Spokane so I can host you on my show. I was just one of hundreds of people to email them after their BBC interview. They responded and said they wanted to come, but that U.S. customs refused to issue them a visa.

I told them to hold on, and I would see what I could do. I went to Breean Beggs (who was the director of the Center for Justice at the time), Lupito at the radio station, and a city council member and asked them all to write letters of support for this couple and their mission to plant a peace tree in our city. It worked! Jafar and Nasim were issued visas, and they rode their bicycles all the way from Toronto to Spokane.

In addition to coming on the radio show, *The Spokesman-Review* did a huge front-page article on them. We also had a gathering of dozens of cyclists to celebrate Jafar and Nasim, their journey, and this amazing opportunity for cultural exchange. We all rode our bikes to Polly Judd Park and planted the peace tree. Jafar and Nasim then went to the city council and thanked them and did presentations at three different schools and at the Community Building lobby about their country and their journey. When they finally went back to Iran after their world tour, they invited me to bring some of my listeners to visit them. A year later, on the anniversary of planting a tree in Spokane, six of my listeners planted a tree in Iran.

Because of this radio station and the opportunity to make my voice heard, I was able to connect with a global community and, together, create beautiful experiences and hope for a wonderful future. This anecdote illustrates that the impacts at the CBC are immense and immeasurable, and that through every story we tell, we empower and inspire more and more people—both on and off the air.

CHAPTER TEN

Launching a Food Co-op with Developer Capital

By Megan White

Megan served in various management positions at Main Market Food Co-op for ten years. She's currently working on an urban permaculture production and teaching farm on her home property in Spokane.

Main Market Co-op is a beautiful grocery and deli in the heart of Spokane. It has over six thousand members, which means the membership has grown by 700% over the past ten years. It is the only mission-driven grocery in the city, and it provides wholesome, responsibly sourced food. It strives to be a socially responsible employer and is a vibrant part of the downtown area and our larger Spokane community. With equal respect for consumers, producers, and the environment, Main Market strives to offer the highest quality with the smallest footprint while growing the strength of the local food system. It's here to sell groceries, but it pledges to do that in a way that cares for all of our community and makes us stronger together.

How we were able to carry out our mission while I was there was deeply influenced by where our start-up capital came from, how quickly we jumped from conception to construction to being open for business, and what downstream effects came from our early organizational structure.

A produce display at Main Market Co-op

I was at Main Market when we opened the doors in 2010. I started as a produce stocker, moved to manager of produce, then store manager, and was hired as the fifth and longest-lasting general manager to date in 2013. I transitioned to finance manager in 2018 and left for good recently to make way for new leadership and to pursue other passions.

When Jim Sheehan bought the old Goodyear Tire store in 2008 and decided to turn it into a food co-op, he hired a team of people to manage the project. His expertise was much more in the nonprofit and service realm, but he had a passion for slow food, noticed there was no food co-op in Spokane, and observed that the local food economy seemed sluggish. There were several local farmer's markets, but Jim's vision was to create a permanent food hub, a place where people could organize and really influence the local food economy. Within eighteen months of purchasing the building, he assembled a team, put up the financing, and got out of the way so they could get to work.

The team he assembled excelled at generating community excitement. They got local organizations invested and news outlets on board. They did an incredible job of capitalizing on the public spotlight. A lot of members signed up in a short period of time, and they couldn't wait to have a food co-op in Spokane. Communities smaller than Spokane had really healthy co-ops, and since the State of Washington is such a food hub for the entire country, it made a lot of sense to try to source more local food together. A lot of the media focused on how cool the building was and on the extracurricular activities like farm tours and volunteer opportunities. The whole idea of improving the local food economy felt vital, imminent, and possible.

Within a few days of opening, it was clear the co-op was going to have some long-term problems. First, we only had products from a few local farmers on the shelves. Granted, it was January—not a good time to launch a local product-focused food store in the Northwest—but it was hard to differentiate our selection and see evidence of our mission on the shelves. Also, in the rush of meeting our opening date, our cashiers had not been fully trained, which caused long lines and long waits. In produce, as in most of the rest of the store, the retail execution was messy. The inventory wasn't entered well in the register system, and none of the produce had price tags, so cashiers couldn't enter their prices manually. Finally, the sticker shock of being a small retail store in a mega-store world was irreversible. Within our first week, we had been branded as the most expensive grocery store in Spokane. People saw us as a boutique specialty food store instead of a home-grown co-op supporting local farmers.

Many people seemed to feel let down when they visited the store for the first time, and sales performance quickly made that observation real. That opening performance, combined with the stress of adjusting plans, caused a lot of the relationships the team had invested in as they built toward the grand opening to suffer. People were disappointed by high prices, lack of product on the shelf, and lack of local products. Quickly, operating losses started to skyrocket, and we had to adjust staffing. The resulting employee turnover was an unbearable blow to morale.

A general manager transition quickly happened, and our board struggled to maintain control and keep the store open. When I became produce manager shortly after this time, I learned even more about the mistakes that were made— using expensive vendors, not getting pricing or store design guidance from experts, not following some critical parts of the professional market study advice that we had paid a substantial amount of money to get. Ten years later, Main Market is still trying to recover from these challenges that would have been mitigated by taking time to train and utilize expert national resources before opening.

One big blind spot was a focus on innovation over best practices. The focus was much more on a big, beautiful building than on business planning and engaging the many national cooperative retail experts available. It's really challenging to balance stewarding a vision with incorporating feedback from other organizations, but embracing professional opinions is a huge part of laying the foundation for a successful enterprise. The building design is not in line with best practices for co-ops or grocery stores; and from what I've been able to put together, nearly all professional consultation that was formally or informally sought came from people in Spokane.

There was a dangerously fine line between being innovative and trying too hard to reinvent retail and grocery. The original team took risks that were cool and interesting, but they ended up being a big liability over time. The project design was skewed toward innovation, without enough expert feedback as I came to learn later when bringing in national consultants to help us re-work our space. Downstream, this caused heavy loss of cash and layout issues that have never translated well to grocery and have always been confusing to customers.

A great example of innovation over practicality is the original freezer lockers. At the time, meat lockers were seeing a resurgence in urban areas as demand increased for purchasing ethically raised meats at a good price. A good price is more easily achieved when buying in bulk, so customers in places like New York City started renting freezer space to store their large cuts of organic beef. But in a city like Spokane where the population density is 3,526 people per square mile (versus 27,000 people per square mile in New York), having freezer locker rentals line the whole north end of the store generated interest but was an administrative nightmare and ate into valuable frozen retail sales space that was not meeting customer needs. It was a huge upfront investment that we quickly had to discontinue, and it would have cost $30,000 to convert to retail space.

Another example was the state-of-the-art greenhouse on the roof. It's a really cool idea, but running a greenhouse is a completely different operation than running a grocery store. It had additional start-up costs aside from the physical greenhouse, and it required a well-trained manager to run. For a while, the greenhouse became a PR nightmare since everyone could see it was empty up there, and it made it seem like we weren't appropriately managing our resources—even though scaling back and focusing on profitability and cash-flow issues was exactly what we needed to do. Focusing on the greenhouse in our beginning crisis was impossible as it would have detracted from other important aspects of scaling. I think an outside consultant would have suggested that it's hard to have a successful retail business and to simultaneously run a full greenhouse operation.

In hindsight, the real innovation that the co-op should have focused on was supporting local farmers and connecting the community to food and local farms. The space, location, and accessibility are all important. Shoppers loved the beautiful building and café, and they were excited that it was sustainably built. But as national consultants quickly confirmed, things like freezer lockers, color schemes, and light fixtures—aspects of the building that received a lot of attention—are less important than executing excellent retail and meeting member shopping needs on price and product. The store's location and accessibility were also a challenge. While it was innovative to have a grocery in downtown far from higher density residential living, the minimal parking and accessibility to our downtown residents didn't match up with a locally focused grocery store. Our deli ended up being the more popular focus of downtown folks but was designed far too small and took much longer to find its niche as we adjusted the business model. A popular saying in the co-op grocery model is "no margin, no mission" and that has been especially true for us. Inability to make money through the retail grocery store and deli cut off our ability to be a good employer and follow through on our promises to our local farmers and members.

The next step was starting over in as many areas as we could. We reached out to people we should have been deeply tied to at the beginning: a group called National Co+op Grocers (NCG). NCG helps unify food co-ops in order to optimize operational and marketing resources, strengthen purchasing power, and ultimately offer more value to food co-op shoppers everywhere. NCG strongly advised us to make a lot of changes, which were ultimately good for the business but were hard to put in place since we weren't designed that way from the beginning. They had us decrease our retail floor space by shutting down and relocating bulk, which was very difficult for shoppers to understand. The perception was that we were decreasing needed inventory, when in reality our store size is much too large for the current or potential sales volume we can attain. They, of course, wanted us to convert the freezer lockers to retail but knew we simply didn't have the capital to pull it off. While they thought the building was beautiful and very nicely designed, they agreed with what we quickly learned in that first year: The store was hard for customers to navigate, the deli and café were too small, and the checkout stands and retail space were not well laid out.

We first met with NCG in 2013 and starting seriously applying their recommendations after they audited our store in 2014. They assessed our strengths and weaknesses and helped us make plans. At that point we started to understand the challenges of lack of store-adjacent parking and distance from a residential neighborhood. With our downtown clientele and convention goers milling around just one block away, NCG helped us realize that the deli was going to be the cornerstone of our operation, and we were lucky to finally find a deli manager who could help evolve our model. NCG helped us meld the creative vision for the space with expertise in national trends. In 2014, food co-ops were deep in what the sector had started to call "the new normal," which refers to the fact that co-ops were no longer the only place to buy organic. Until our audit, we were looking at the downward trend of sales and wondering, what in the world is going on?

It wasn't until we connected to the national conversation that we realized the entire cooperative grocery sector was experiencing this kind of crisis, competing with businesses that had way more scale. It's been our experience that, with the rise of the new normal, generally only the most committed co-op shoppers care where they purchase their organic produce. Many shoppers assume all organic product is created equally, and most find large corporate stores more accessible to choose buying organically with only some of their product choices. It's beautiful that co-ops have created this demand for organics because changing demand changes the world. But the mission of food co-ops runs much deeper than just sourcing organics, and when customers choose to buy their organic produce from Main Market, they are voting with their dollars for a healthy, local, sustainable food system and a co-operative structure that keeps dollars in the community.

One of the hardest lessons I've learned over the years is that a membership-based ownership model will always struggle to retain and grow membership if it's financed with 100% developer capital. If you don't need to depend on membership support to open your doors, it's excruciatingly difficult to mobilize those members after the project has launched. It's such a known risk, in fact, that NCG viewed our application for membership as higher risk because of it—in addition, of course, to our high losses and limitations in cash in our first few years. There's always a trade-off. No matter which kind of co-op you are, everyone is looking at the other and saying, what a beautiful building or, I'd love to have your fridge, while we're saying, look at your 70%-member shopping rate—we'd love to have that. Start-up capital is much harder to come by, but the power in numbers and commitment to make something succeed long-term is much more important.

In my final years at the co-op, a key strategy for long-term success that we were working to improve was affordability, which was not clearly emphasized when we opened. Membership cost $180, and the cheapest payment plan was $60 all at once. This cost was realistic for the people who signed up before we opened, but not at all realistic for the surrounding community that lacked access to a close grocery store when the last true downtown grocer closed years ago. We saw the largest surge in membership when we switched to a $10 annual equity payment plan. This was the magic number where people said yeah, we can afford that, or yeah, we'll sign up. Thanks to our relationship with NCG, we were also able to source products more affordably, and we passed those saving on to our customers and members. We also instituted a very popular $3 dinner night once per week to try to reach out to more of our community. There are still struggles, even though the co-op's prices are now cheaper on key products than anywhere else in town. But whether it's this beautiful building that's created too nice of an image, or the fact that we're all organic (which is perceived as more expensive), or the historic branding from when we first opened, the slow growth and low margin inherent in any grocery model has made it hard to overcome the financial challenges we had early on. The good news is that the co-op is still going strong, continues to work hard for growth, and is always learning from and responding to customers.

During my time there, we were working to have a better handle on who our customers really were. Three different groups have a relationship with us: convention goers, a core group of mission supporters, and block dwellers. Convention goers come to the store for the good deli and healthy food, and they often repeat each year. We value those customers, and the booms from conventions provide a 10% to 15% increase in revenue annually, which helps see us through leaner times. But the convention goers don't have a relationship with how we started or who we are.

Thankfully, there's also a core group in Spokane that became customers when we opened in 2010 and is growing with some of the migration from Seattle and Portland, as well as from locals responding to our hard work. These members could get organic anywhere in town, but they want to belong to a co-op because they understand the deeper mission and the greater responsibility we have with food. They are coming to the co-op as a values-driven choice and voting with their dollars.

Finally, there are the block dwellers and immediate downtown community who shop here out of convenience and enjoy the vitality the co-op brings to the block. The co-op brings together diverse and intersecting groups of people. It's interesting to me how often I see people having incidental but meaningful encounters. Food provides a connection point for people across a city. That's what I like to see the most. The co-op is a destination for people with a particular ideology, but it also brings in a robust cross-section of the city that generates a more diverse sense of our community than you might find in any single building on the block. I've always loved that food is a common language and connection point for all the diversity of our city and country.

Any other strategy for long-term success came from educating ourselves as much as possible about what we really were. For a long time, we had a confused identity about not only who we were trying to serve, but also who we were as a company. We didn't have a personnel handbook when we opened, human resource practices and procedures were unclear, there was no system for accountability, and no one save the GM and bookkeeper was trained on finances or how to run a business. No one was training new employees in what a co-op is or training managers on how to spend or manage personnel costs. For the first few years, the leadership looked to Jim to figure out what he wanted, and in this way became financially dependent on him, too. Jim made it clear that he built and owned the building, but he wanted it to be the community's co-op. However, it was hard to figure out what the community's co-op should look like after the initial debacle around opening and repeated GM turnovers. I asked for a loan to get us out of crisis management mode, which we were in for so long, and which doesn't give you much time to figure out who you are or envision a clear path to sustainability.

The loan gave us the chance to survive while we made a new plan, which mostly meant learning everything we could from NCG. They gave us a lot of training resources and a great deal of free and low-cost consulting. They visited the store and helped us find our identity and serve the community better. They provided significant educational training about what it means to be a cooperative and how to embrace a cooperative identity. But to be honest, finances were the number one thing that we focused on in our quest to become members with NCG and work toward sustainability. Since we struggled to open well and lost so much money, profitability, and customers early on, we had to figure out how to make money work before we worked on anything else. 2016 was the first year that asking Jim for money was not an emergency business necessity as we started to see our planning and hard work pay off. We are still paying down our loans and will be for a long time, but that loan repayment is now part of a sustainable business plan, and we have a lot more ingredients for success moving forward.

Megan White, longtime contributor to Main Market Co-op and its success

Around when I left, with the financial piece more firmly in place, we were focusing on priorities that should have happened the first year we opened. We were investing in getting people to understand membership and ownership, getting more farmers plugged in, and doing more for the local food economy. The co-op continues to do more education internally and externally. It felt good after many years to be thinking less about survival and more about our mission.

My number one recommendation I have from these last ten years is don't lose sight of best practices in your desire to innovate. In hindsight, the grand conceptual plans for the co-op didn't all connect or make sense to what should have been the central retail focus, and there were a lot of unintended consequences downstream of those attempts to innovate.

Innovation did attract the most attention, but it never translated into a good bottom line financially that could then feed the mission. From the beginning we tried to do too much at once: operate a greenhouse on the roof, manage a full composting station on the back of our building, organize farm tours and local food dinners. When the pressure of running a struggling retail operation arose, these innovations became impossible to manage.

Another insight is don't be innovative everywhere. Pick one or two focus areas and make sure you're covering all the realities, too. By the time we opened our doors, people expected a tropical greenhouse with full rooftop garden, weekly volunteer opportunities, weekly classes, bags of compost being sold on our retail floor, and local harvest on every shelf. That was a lot of expectations to manage and impossible to do all at once; it disappointed members and lost us customers.

I also noticed that the co-op has always felt different from the other projects on the Community Building Campus. The rest of the campus evolved and scaled more organically. And Jim, the visionary, had a lot more experience with social and environmental justice than he had with the local food economy. When launching the Community Building, Jim didn't start with the building. He first founded the Center for Justice and started looking for a permanent home for his nonprofit. The building was a natural progression, a next step, and all the innovation that ensued seemed to be more in relationship, more of an ecosystem. With the co-op, the innovation seemed to be front-ended rather than a creative take on an intuitive next step. After looking at the history of many co-ops across the country, I believe leadership initially lost sight of one of its founding community-building principles: let community build organically. Had we followed that advice, the co-op would have a very different history.

But the positive part of a developer-owned co-op (which is rarer with a community-minded philanthropic developer like Jim) is the emergency infusions of cash in the form of low-interest loans to get you through a hard place. To Jim's credit, he never abandoned the project despite its start-up challenges; as a person and as a leader, he is loyal, and he never wants anyone or any project to fail. His long-term commitment gave us time to evolve, seek out best practices, and put in place a sustainable, community-centered business model. It took us some time to stop asking—What does Jim want?—and to start realizing that he ultimately wanted what the community needed, and it was our responsibility to use his start-up resources to figure that out.

I'm sure Main Market is still learning and becoming the co-op that Spokane needs. It now solicits more feedback and is more tuned in to the needs of members, and leadership is more forthcoming about the financial challenges of running a complicated retail store. The store is also more in sync with national trends, and it's not trying to solve these problems on its own since it can rely on the experts at NCG for guidance. Main Market is also looking at its role as the only grocery store in the downtown core, and how it can potentially support low-income members of our community through programs like WIC—even if some of the products offered through those programs don't strictly fulfill the mission of stocking responsibly-sourced foods.

There is no perfect answer, no perfect co-op, within the greater context of a food system driven by corporations and profit. Trying to balance our love of people, stewardship of the planet, and need for a sustainable profit is a constant challenge, and it always will be. That's why the innovation Main Market is striving for today is not so grand as it was at the co-op's launch; in fact, it may be imperceptible to many. Today's innovation is a gradual change based on consistently soliciting feedback from the community and incrementally making change—and learning how to evolve our early challenges into unique successes. Just like the farmers and growers the co-op supports, it is an organization operating within a greater, complicated ecosystem. The only way for it to maintain sustainable operations for the long term is to strive for this consistent, incremental evolution.

CHAPTER ELEVEN

Global Fair Trade and the Local Economy

Part One by Denise Attwood

Denise is the founder of Ganesh Himal Trading Company, which directly imports high-quality, handcrafted clothing, jewelry, textiles, and paper from small cottage industries in Nepal. Her business is based in Spokane, and she was one of the original champions of fair trade in the region, before it even had a name.

When I cover myself with a hand-woven blanket and feel the richness of the maker's skill and care, I feel the warmth of humanity wash over me. The flicker of a candle in a hand-hewn copper holder with skillfully carved flowers casts patterns into the dark spaces of my room, and I feel heartened and connected to the artisan and his or her love of craft. The hand-tatted table covering exemplifies the love and care of one who knows this craft so well and can share its ancient roots directly with me without even uttering a word. This is the human beauty, dignity, and soul that we cannot afford to lose in these times when we feel so separate and alone. These items of beauty, of our humanity, link us back to each other.

What I am talking about here has become known by the term fair trade. What constitutes fair trade? In our version, all partnerships are grounded in reciprocity. We work diligently to establish mutually beneficial relationships with our producers in Nepal by encouraging a balanced level of give and take.

Denise Attwood, founder of Ganesh Himal Trading Company

We work directly with producers as a team, expanding each other's talents and ideas. We believe everyone's insight and perspective is needed to create systems that address the changing nature of our world.

And what do we lose if we no longer hold in our hands the richness of a handmade work, if we no longer hear in our mind the distant clacking of the treadles of a loom, or see the gentle thoughtfulness expressed on the face of the one creating the next stitch on an intricate pattern? What happens if we lose this? We disconnect with the timeline of humanity that passes this knowing from one generation to the next. We lose that deep sense of how we need each other to survive. We feel more separate and alone.

Fair trade is about regenerating the value of intimate relationships through acknowledging the reciprocal exchange of the gifts that we all have—and putting that energy in motion. It helps us all to lead fuller, richer, and more beautiful lives. When I work with an artisan who with her hands creates an item that is not only beautiful but helpful to me, and I exchange with her an expression of the depth of respect that I have for her talent, the gratitude that she provides for me is something that I cannot provide for myself. If I compensate her labor in an amount that values and respects her life energy, then there is beauty in that exchange, and a circle of interconnectivity that provides for all our needs. If I then bring that item to a person in North America and let that person experience her beauty and the richness she brings to the world through her craft, I make a connection of human energy and love far beyond just the exchange of money for an object. That chain of connection is beauty in raw form, and it allows for a touching of souls across continents that I believe gives us a deep hope for our shared future. This interaction, through trade, helps us to remember why we are here on this beautiful planet.

Fair trade is also about the gentle rebalancing of power through respect and redistribution, while acknowledging our deep human need to be connected. Nature always is providing us with examples of how energy is reciprocal, that life is always giving to more life, and that in order for life to flourish, there must be balance. If I breathe out carbon dioxide, the trees and plants receive it and return to me the life-giving oxygen that allows me to survive. Together, our actions are mutually beneficial and life giving. Neither action is more valuable than the other, but both are needed for life to be maintained. Fair trade is a reciprocal, balanced exchange that acknowledges at the deepest level our need for each other and the gifts that each of us bring to the other. When trade is approached from that deep sense of reciprocity and relationship, it moves us all toward beauty, balance, and right relationship.

Kim played such an important role in fair trade in Spokane. She brought people in and helped them understand their value in being a participant in this just economy. She was so conscious and attentive. People left Kizuri feeling more connected, more inspired, and more hopeful, which drew them back. Her approach was a good business tactic, since people can see through inauthenticity, and they subconsciously feel good in the presence of business owners who are truly engaged. Fair trade speaks from a place of the heart. It starts from creating and maintaining relationships with our products and it continues into creating and maintaining relationships with customers. Relationships are our heartbeat. Fair trade alone will not save the world, but it definitely opens our hearts. It is one of the pieces of the puzzle that helps us walk each other home to the remembering of why we are here on this beautiful planet and what brings us deeply into love.

Part Two by Kim Harmson

Kim Harmson is the founder of Kizuri, a vibrant, community-inspired fair trade store. She is an early childhood educator and got her start in fair trade volunteering at Global Folk Art with her two children in the early '90s.

Behind the muted greens and maroons of the Community Building's street front, color and light radiate from behind the tall glass windows. Clusters of large stars illuminate the vibrant display and cast a whimsical light over products from all over the world. Felted garland balls wind around soft piles of hand-stitched cotton throws from India. Scattered about the shop are locally crafted soaps, hand-dipped candles, textiles from Guatemala, jewelry from Nepal, goblets and bowls of wildly colored glass—and a unique vibe that draws people in to experience the light, the textures, and the stories.

What sets Kizuri apart from other retail environments is the intentionality that infuses every aspect of our enterprise. While most vendors talk about supply chains, we focus on relationships. Our relationships with customers, artisans, and the environment make all the difference. Those beautiful, one-of-a-kind, hand-woven throws provide employment in one of the poorest areas of India. Workers are guaranteed training, a safe work environment, and fair wages so they can provide for themselves and their families. The pure beeswax candles are clean burning and release negative ions that improve air quality by eliminating pollutants and allergens. The popular Hebron Glass has been a family-owned business in the West Bank since 1890. To make these stunning pieces of functional art, recycled glass is smashed into pieces and melted in high-temperature ovens to create unique colors and patterns.

Shoppers stand at the checkout of Kizuri

Photo by Rajah Bose

During my time running the shop in the Community Building, I had one job but many roles. At a very task-oriented level, I was the founder and owner, and like most small business owners, I juggled a million things at once. I had to multitask or pivot suddenly because there are so many elements to having a small business. If the computer broke down, I was the IT person. Sometimes I'd be busy with a customer and a huge order would come in. With limited storage space, it was necessary to unpack and display inventory right away. I had one wonderful woman, Jennifer, who worked in the shop two days a week for the last nine years, but otherwise I managed everything on the front and back ends.

I called myself the orchestrator at Kizuri because my role was so dynamic, and the term seemed to encompass all my roles: the expected ones, and those I stepped into unknowingly. Kizuri seems to me a living organism that has evolved over time, influenced by all the people that come through the doors of the Community Building. My goal was to provide fair trade products of exceptional beauty that people use in their day-to-day lives, which means another one of my roles was curator of functional art: cookware hand-formed with clay from the Magdalena River in Colombia, beautiful woven textiles (tablecloths, napkins, rugs) from women in Nepal, exquisite hand-embroidered embellishments on stylish clothing, bowls and utensils carved from sustainable wood. And baskets!

I was so inspired after spending time with women basket weavers in Rwanda. They harvest and shred the natural fibers to create single strands that they then dye in big boiling vats of brightly colored water. The fibers are dried in their homes, gardens, or workshops until it is time to sit with their sisters to weave together—colorful strand by colorful strand, day by day. Often these baskets find their place as cherished decorative wall art. But they are also highly durable and functional as bread baskets, plant pots, market baskets, laundry hampers, and receptacles for everyday necessities or found treasures.

In addition to being a purveyor of fair trade goods, I became a community educator. When I first met a customer, I thought about planting seeds. I might say, my gosh, I met the people who wove this basket, and then I'd give the customer just a piece of the story—a little spark. If I saw someone lingering over an object, I would try to intuit if he wanted to talk more. If people were open to a conversation, we had enriching and meaningful exchanges, though sometimes just a warm welcome to the store was enough. The role that fair trade plays in our global environment sparked many conversations as well. Most of us are aware that there is too much trash on the earth, so shoppers are excited to hear stories about artisans repurposing materials, like the recycled tire bags we sell from Nepal. In Kathmandu, there is a tremendous amount of trash that is burned daily, which deteriorates air quality to extremely unhealthy standards. The recycled tires used to create these bags divert this material from the waste stream. They have become so popular with conscious consumers and young shoppers that the producer co-op in Nepal now hires people to venture into the countryside specifically to find more tires to create more bags.

Personally, I have never been a big shopper or collector, but I think there's a way to weave fair trade into one's life that is not about acquiring more and more stuff. It invites a shopper to consider the impact her purchase makes—the impact on the life of the person who produced the product, the environmental impact of how the item was produced, and whether or not the materials used are recycled or sustainable. I have always searched for things that are beautiful, functional, and have a story to tell. I have also thought a lot about where we are here in the Northwest and how a piece of beautiful art from Africa fits into our regional environment. Color is a big consideration. I've found that blues and greens sell better in Spokane. The store strives to maintain a sense of balance representing rich, global color palettes of faraway places, but what sells most here at Kizuri are the colors of the Northwest-earth, foliage, and sky.

I have always loved the mission of fair trade, but I never considered owning my own shop until a need appeared in our community. I was working part time with my good friends at Ganesh Himal Trading—a wholesale distributor of fair trade products from Nepal—while doing educational consulting in 2008. Global Folk Art, Spokane's volunteer-run fair trade store since the late '90s, was struggling financially and decided to close its doors for good. As Denise and I talked about this at work one morning, I realized that I couldn't accept losing our only fair trade presence in Spokane and decided to create another store in Global's place.

Global Folk Art only had the resources to fund a part-time manager at about eighteen hours a week. Realistically, that is not enough time to address all the essential operations, let alone the attention necessary to keep the store continually evolving and vibrant. I decided to commit to the project full-time, giving me the opportunity to explore new projects and products, build relationships with customers and wholesalers, rotate displays, promote the business, and give more time to outreach and education. I also did a lot of research and gleaned valuable information from other fair trade stores around the country.

I wrote a very nontraditional business plan on handmade Nepali paper using language that made sense to me illustrating my passion, commitment, and intentions. And then I called Jim and asked if he would meet with me to talk about my dream. I took my little business plan to his office and told him that I wanted to run a new fair trade store in the Global Folk Art space. I explained my mission to him: to create a vibrant, sustainable, community-oriented shop that offered unsurpassed customer service. I planned to feature quality gifts and clothes at affordable prices that were fairly traded, earth friendly, or locally produced. I wanted to support positive and ethical work environments and fair trade practices, and I was also determined to give back to the local community.

I walked away from that meeting knowing that I had the space for my business, but I had two main concerns. One was that all the organizations in the Community Building at that time were nonprofits, and I didn't want to be a nonprofit. I wanted to be a for-profit business inspired by nonprofit principles, like operating for the public good, and I certainly didn't want to bring everything to a board each time I needed to make a major decision. That was initially a big concern, which I realized later wasn't really an obstacle at all. I could launch a mission-driven business in our community with Jim's encouragement and support. Rather than a board, I organized a group of friends and mentors to advise me when I needed or desired outside input. It was very informal and worked perfectly. I simply reached out when I wanted inspiration and feedback.

Kizuri's founder, Kim Harmson

I do still keep in touch with many of them.

My second concern about starting Kizuri was a big one: I didn't have the money to make it happen. I asked for a second meeting with Jim to see if he would be involved in funding my enterprise, and to my delight, he said yes. He committed to lending me a chunk of the money I needed, and anything over that amount I had to raise. Jim believed in the project and said yes, but he also said the enterprise had to be bigger than just the two of us—it must involve the greater community. I sent letters to friends, and talked to neighbors and anyone who would listen. They, in turn, talked to their friends. Eventually, we were able to gather the funding through long-term, low-interest loans from ten other members of our community, and I never had to go to a bank. Over the years, Global Folk Art had built a community of people committed to fair trade, and they came together and made Kizuri possible. I paid off the last of my community financing in 2014, but most of the loans were paid off within eighteen months as Kizuri exceeded initial income projections—even though we opened in October of 2008 when the market crashed.

I love that Kizuri is essentially a community space in many other ways, too. As the first presence visitors encounter in the Community Building, I served as a guide, helping people find the Center for Justice on the third floor or other organizations in the warren of offices and meeting rooms on our campus. When Kizuri's decorative iron doors are open during business hours, the lobby becomes an extension of the store, and vice versa: colorful displays of baskets and clothing tumble forth, and people naturally drift in—some to shop, some to fill their senses with beautiful treasures, and some stop by to visit. Parents of toddlers from the Community Building Children's Center pop in to buy a gift for a loved one before picking up their kids from school. The Spokane Riverkeeper films updates about its programs against the colorful backdrop of our storefront. Students from Riverside High School have come to our store year after year on field trips to learn about fair trade. We always enjoy the chance meetings and greetings in our permeable space and the many relationships we have formed with visitors and fellow tenants alike.

Fortunately, the story of the next phase of Kizuri is as serendipitous as its start. Five years ago, I met a woman named Jillian Joseph while my husband and I were in Rwanda on our first medical mission with a group called Healing Hearts Northwest. Jillian had grown up in Spokane and was living in Paris at the time. She came to Rwanda to hang out with her parents who are friends of ours and were on the same mission in Rwanda.

Jillian and I found we had some down time, and so I invited her to shop with me for Kizuri, which I did whenever I traveled. We visited women's co-ops in small, remote villages and in some of the more bustling areas of Kigali. Jillian had lived in Senegal and was very comfortable moving through Africa. I thought to myself, this young woman would be just perfect at Kizuri. We kept in touch, and several years later when I learned that she was returning to Washington, I decided to plant the seed and see what would come of it. I suggested to Jillian she should consider the possibilities of taking over Kizuri when she got back to Spokane. I had managed Kizuri for ten years and was feeling it was time for me to consider retirement and shift my attention to grandchildren and travel. We first connected by phone and then via email, and I could tell the idea was starting to take hold.

Jillian has a compassionate heart, a strong work ethic, and a feisty spirit that is continually working for social justice and equality in our neighborhoods and throughout the world—not to mention a darn good eye for products of beauty, quality, and function. The fact that she is younger automatically gives the store a renewed sense of vibrancy and longevity. But it's no secret that I cried after the transition became official. I have spent so many wonderful days developing relationships with local vendors, international co-ops, customers that have become friends, and the amazing people at the Community Building that it's impossible to leave the day-to-day work without feeling a lot of emotion.

Perhaps my most fulfilling role as orchestrator at Kizuri was being involved in the everyday lives of my neighbors on the block. I miss those daily connections, the vibrancy of my neighborhood, and the intentionality of all the work that people do there. It was very purposeful, satisfying, and creative. Even now I feel my primary work was being in that space and having a relationship with everyone who came through it. It was a privilege and filled my soul to listen to people's stories, brainstorm ideas together, share the joys and sorrows of life, to have a moment to frolic with the kids in the lobby, or merely assist people with directions. All of this is in the spirit of fair trade, which—at its core—is about how interconnected and woven through each other's lives we are.

Part Two

Community Building Is a Verb

CHAPTER TWELVE

Capacity Building: The Foundation's Role

By Patty Gates

Patty served as the executive director of the Community Building Foundation. She invested deeply in her role as ambassador and champion for nonprofits and their staff for fifteen years.

In 1999, Jim hired me to facilitate his family's philanthropic projects, naming the effort the Community Building Foundation (CBF). The physical space—the Community Building—had been created, and the Center for Justice had been launched. Jim and his family discussed the impact of the philanthropic arm of the effort as being both a noun, in terms of the physical space, as well as a verb, creating positive changes in the community. The role of their foundation in the overall enterprise is to both build community and unity among tenants in the building and to carry the Community Building mission into the greater Spokane region. In other words, the CBF actively supports the verb aspect of the mission, the deeply relational and ongoing work of building community.

It's impossible to talk about the foundation's work without first describing Jim's unique approach to philanthropy and leadership. He was known for saying, "I want people to experience justice in Spokane. You're on my team, so go make that happen in the best, most effective ways you can." His signature value, "It's all about relationships," allowed me to move into my role as executive director by building upon the well-established relationships and connections I had created personally and professionally over my twenty-five years in Spokane as a third-grade teacher and a staff developer at Franklin Elementary School. Being tasked with "building community" with this kind of trust and freedom was both energizing and humbling. Not many bosses invite their employees to explore their own strengths and intuitions in such an open and creative environment. Being able to go where my strengths and interests pulled me, within the parameters of the foundation's mission, allowed me to do my best work. For me, this meant growing fully into my role as a connector, ambassador, and champion as well as co-worker.

In my work at the CBF, I learned that one of the beauties of philanthropy is that it can be a highly creative process. While there is no "one size fits all" approach that ensures success, there is a more flexible framework for creating lasting change. In my experience with foundation work, the most important ingredients for success are building strong relationships, a commitment to the underlying values, and an openness to what is possible. Focusing on capacity building allowed us to consistently and dynamically apply these ingredients, and the CBF supported the capacity of dozens of organizations and became an integral part of hosting, inspiring, and catalyzing social change in the Spokane region. We are not the only institution to do philanthropy in this way, but we were early adopters and have twenty years of experience in this hands-off, relationship-driven approach.

Over time, I began to see my primary role as a connector, someone who could track the many layers of nonprofit projects and the leaders who could enhance them. My greatest joy was introducing people who had a shared vision or who had the potential for creating one.

Capacity Building to Support Organizational Leaders

Strong relationships don't start on day one. I may have been introduced to someone at a meeting or fundraising event. Then we'd schedule a conversation over coffee so I could learn more about their passion. Then I might meet their staff and embark on an ongoing relational journey with people fulfilling the mission of that organization. I was there to observe in order to learn about them personally and professionally and to see what the board members were excited about.

Patty Gates, former executive director of the Community Building Foundation

In some cases, I supported the organization as another staff person. At times, I would help with troubleshooting organizational challenges, or I would serve in an advisory role, or as a collaborator. I attended board and staff meetings, depending on need and relationship. Generally, for larger and ongoing grants, the relationship was much more in depth. For other organizations, we had a more traditional relationship and purchased a table at an auction or attended events.

Our work was always centered on relationships and personal connection, no matter what the goal or outcome was. We discovered that if our relationship was healthy and strong, the likelihood of success was probable. Of course, projects still struggled, and organizations went through the growing pains common to nonprofits. But because building strong relationships was our goal, it allowed us to support a different, more holistic outcome. Supporting progressive social change is a long-term investment, and investing in the relationships of organizations and leadership is critical to the scope of long-term work.

This belief was powerful to me, and it has become my personal mantra: It's all about the relationship. Most people working in nonprofits, especially leadership, are excited about their work, so it's pretty easy to get started on that level of shared excitement. Connecting personally around an idea is what sparked it for me, a big part of what made it work. A lot of funders, by design, don't develop a personal relationship with grantees or don't articulate a focus on relationships. But the CBF board understood that when you really work well with people and you have resources to support their ideas, amazing things can happen. Believing in the human spirit is a powerful impetus for achieving visions. As we moved toward those visions, the foundation's relationships with grantees—as well as the monetary support—became a conduit toward achieving those goals.

Another way to talk about our work at the foundation is as capacity builders. Our grants were never very large, ranging between $2,000 and $15,000. It made sense for us to invest in an organization in a variety of additional ways. One of the primary roles I filled in my job as director was to be available to the organizations we funded in order to strengthen their capacity for success.

Creating capacity for a nonprofit means ensuring that the infrastructure is robust enough for the organization to fulfill its mission. Some examples of this are building a strong cadre of volunteers, ensuring an effective communications strategy with current technology, staff development, and succession planning. A $10,000 grant to a small nonprofit can do a lot toward keeping the doors open and the lights on, or to fund a particular project. But my availability as a member of the grantee's "team" in terms of strategizing for success, working on committees, and connecting the organization to others who could further their mission could do even more. Being able to contribute personally to the community building of the foundation by using the full expression of my intuition and talents was deeply rewarding. I knew every day that Jim's inheritance was serving as a conduit for the values he and his team wanted to express through the foundation and the Center for Justice: connection and justice, and the nourishment of community, beauty, and love.

Capacity Building through Love: Neighborhood Outreach

As director of the Community Building Foundation, and with the help of many volunteers from the organizations in the buildings, we organized several events designed to bring tenants and our neighbors together. A quarterly Saturday breakfast for neighbors who used the services of the nearby homeless shelters was a way to provide food, get to know each other, and offer connections to services such as legal advice, shelter, and bus passes. Our building became a positive environment in which to connect with people who frequented our block.

These events were also about creating an opportunity for tenants to do something completely outside of their daily activities as a group and to focus together on a community project. Our monthly community potlucks served the same function in a much less formal way. On those days, we transformed the Community Building lobby into a pop up, family-style restaurant where anyone could enjoy a hot cup of coffee and homemade meals. The CBF provided main dishes and drinks, and tenants brought cutlery, plates, and sides. We created the support mechanism to make sure these events happened well, and everyone showed up and participated as they could. Often during the shared lunch, one of the nonprofit leaders from the building would share their organization's background and goals or give an update. This was a way to learn about each other while sharing time and a meal together.

This quarterly endeavor provided the opportunity to step outside the daily demands of running a small nonprofit and focus on a completely different task. This event did not serve any purpose other than bringing people together in an effort to love and serve their community. Nurturing relationships among tenants of the CBC was one of the most important aspects of my job. I also managed the Mac 'n' Cheese Monday program, where a different tenant would present about their organization over a free lunch. There was a time for Q&A and for sharing announcements. But the most important aspect was the opportunity to share a meal, be in the same room, and pay attention to each other's work.

The work of the CBF has evolved over the years, and it is important for funders to let their work evolve. The values of the CBF are strong, and its evolution is a unique blend of who is at the helm, what the community needs, and the ongoing mission of bringing people together.

Capacity Building to Increase Connectivity and Power

The flexibility afforded to me in my role as executive director of the Community Building Foundation allowed me to be nimble and nurture opportunities as they came together. Some of these opportunities included increasing the collective visibility and power of diverse organizations in order to build their capacity.

Photo by Robert Zeller

Patty Gates addressing a roomful of people during a live-streamed Bioneers event

In the traditional sense, building capacity is about creating the framework of an organization so that its mission and values can be felt most effectively in the community. The underlying infrastructure, or capacity, allows the organization to be a force for good. This includes a broad swath of competencies and skills such as team building, visioning, professional development, planning, evaluation, and more. The most successful organizations, ones which have built strong capacities for fulfilling their missions, also demonstrate a high level of social capital. These social competencies include things like strong interpersonal relationships, a shared sense of identity, shared norms and values, trust, cooperation, and reciprocity—both within the organization and with the greater community. It was this area of building social capital that I focused upon in my role as foundation director.

Let me share my experiences with working with two of the grantee organizations of the Community Building Foundation, which reflect the effort to build social capital within the organizations and into the broader community.

Greater Spokane Progress (GSP) was born when a Seattle-based organization called the Win/Win Network approached a few nonprofit leaders in Spokane about investing in progressive issues in Eastern Washington. The goal of Win/Win was to cultivate a civically powerful network in order to advance racial, social, and economic equity and thriving communities across Washington State.

In 2009, the Win/Win Network, which builds dynamic coalitions to increase political participation, asked nonprofit leaders across the CBC to convene a meeting to discuss their expansion to the east side of our state. The infusion of resources from Win/Win paid for a director's position, and more than a dozen Spokane organizations came together to form a progressive organization we named Greater Spokane Progress.

Through this coalition, we learned about each other's efforts and broadened our perspectives. This kind of connectivity and collaboration was already happening in the Community Building, thanks to the proximity of mission-driven organizations. But now we were able to bring together organizations across the city and say, "If you are doing this kind of work, come to the table." And although we had proximity within the Community Building offices, organizational leaders had not carved out a regular time to talk strategy and have greater impact together. Creating this space, to focus on our shared values and relationships, we were able to solidify a broad-based network working for good, which then expanded beyond our doors and into the community.

GSP's interest in increasing collaborations has led to the formation of additional collective priorities that are changing the way organizations work, and work together, in Spokane. The Spokane Progress Plan is a member-designed, goal-oriented action plan that drives their work to transform our region to create a more equitable, peaceful, healthy, and economically and environmentally just community by achieving goals that include: housing justice in Spokane, immigrant and refugee safety and inclusion, and reducing the effects of climate change. Members commit to following through on these goals in their operations and to collectively support campaigns and initiatives that advance these issues.

Another focus area for GSP is helping local organizations use an intersectional racial equity lens through training and support. They coordinate a Racial Equity Trainers' Cohort to lead the training Why Race Matters: History, Systems, and Strategies to develop a collective understanding and common language around institutional and structural racism, and why addressing race matters. Dozens of organizations have participated in this training, including the Spokane Police Department, City staff, and hundreds of community leaders.

Here's another great example of nurturing strategic relationships in the Spokane region: In 2004, Eastern Washington University's Institute for Policy and Economic Analysis commenced the Community Indicators Initiative (CII). This initiative involved the collection of data—or indicators—to assess the state of the Spokane community in terms of economic vitality, education, health, environment, and numerous other factors. A group of community leaders involved in the CII process recognized the value of the indicators for identifying priority community problems and for measuring change on these issues over time. These leaders represented local government, businesses, nonprofit organizations, and local funders. With the vision to prioritize community action to measurably improve the community, these leaders officially launched Priority Spokane in 2008.

In its early days of inception, I was able to be a part of the original steering committee, which helped convene community leader focus groups to determine what data is needed to move the needle toward improving outcomes. Funding from the Community Building Foundation also helped launch the web presence of the project. Bringing people together across a community to address big issues, such as increasing graduation rates, takes intentional focus on creating relationships, prioritizing values, and trusting and cooperating with each other. This was exciting and groundbreaking work that, through targeted and collective interventions, allowed us to increase the graduation rates in Spokane County from 60% to 80% and earned us the Culture of Health Prize from the Robert Wood Johnson Foundation. The effort has also expanded to three Eastern Washington counties beyond Spokane and has become a model for other communities in our state and beyond.

Capacity Building through Funding and Nurturing New Organizations

One of the ways the Community Building Foundation was able to leverage support for smaller, local nonprofits was by providing early financial assistance. One of the most effective questions we asked ourselves when considering funding small start-ups was, "Will this project get off the ground if we don't initiate the funding?" Larger foundations outside of our region are often hesitant to make initial grants to small, locally focused start-ups because they lack the personal contact and experiences with those involved in the work. Because of local funding from the Community Building Foundation and the proximity of the foundation to these local organizations, I was able to share first-hand the successes of projects in our community. When you have personal relationships with the people on the ground doing the work, you know how effective their efforts are. In this role I was able to serve as an ambassador for local nonprofit successes to the larger regional and national funders that helped strengthen their funding requests. This dynamic also played out when the Win/Win Network reached out from Seattle to expand their coalition of successful organizations. They relied on us as a local funding organization to suggest strong nonprofit leaders who should be at the table.

An example of investing in an organization early so that it could get off the ground and then leverage this seed money for more money was the Odyssey Youth Center. The CBF funded them as a start-up to support LGBTQ youth in Spokane. Odyssey then implemented a program started by GLSEN (Gay Lesbian Straight Education Network). GLSEN is a leading national education organization that works to transform K-12 schools into safe and affirming environments and ensure that LGBTQ students are able to learn and grow in a school environment free from bullying and harassment. With funding from CBF, I worked with the director of Odyssey and the Greater Spokane Progress group to make this happen in Spokane. A series of forums for students, educators, parents, and community members explored the need to create a physical space in every Spokane high school where students could meet and support each other. These spaces, called Genders & Sexualities Alliance (GSA), are student-run clubs that provide opportunities to talk about issues related to sexual orientation, gender identity, and expression, and work to end homophobia and transphobia.

In addition to being a funder for the GSA project, the foundation helped facilitate meetings at partner institutions like Gonzaga University and Washington State University. We spent time connecting with parents and teachers on the phone and in person. I was mostly involved in the beginning stages because, once there was a physical space for a safe place to gather, and a teacher volunteering to serve as a liaison, the club could grow depending on what the kids wanted to do with it. Since we started this work in 2012, the whole concept has evolved for the better. There are now more robust efforts in every classroom to be inclusive and supportive of all gender identities.

Capacity Building through Continuity of Support

The continuity of support is hugely important in the life cycle of a nonprofit. For me, continuity meant more than whether the organization could count on a grant check each year. Continuity of support meant that I had relationships with the people in the organizations we served. Year after year, we'd partner for events or work together on campaigns, establishing friendships and connections. We became a part of each other's lives and grew to understand each other's priorities. Friendships span beyond the scope of the "job" and actually redefine what the "job" is. Sharing the physical space helped this to happen, but it was also the Community Building Foundation's mission to see the direct connection between the flowing conduit of our funding and the values we were trying to strengthen in our community.

In addition to the depth of relationship through proximity, the nurturing also came through the inviting and beautiful space that Jim created intentionally. I recall when he began talking about choosing color schemes and furnishings for the buildings. He mused about all the nonprofit spaces he had visited over the years that were housed in dark church basements with poor lighting and old metal filing cabinets in disrepair. In his opinion, the spaces did not fully reflect the efforts and visions that were being created in them. He wanted people to experience the sense of respect and appreciation that a physical space can represent: the work here is good, it matters, and we are committed to doing it.

So, in this beautiful space, organizations became close neighbors. Many of the collaborations were informal, reflective of family living under one roof. In my role as a connector, I was delighted to work in this energetic, vibrant, progressive hive. With such a density of nonprofits and small businesses, it made sense that the Community Building became a hub and a gathering space for the greater community. Similar to being at home, sitting on the front porch, and getting to know our neighbors outside the buildings, we strengthened our ties to our community.

Capacity Building through Intuitive Grant Making: Let it Flow!

Typically, grant making follows a familiar life cycle: A foundation or agency publicizes the grant in a call for proposals, qualifying nonprofits send in their applications, and the funder selects the recipients through internal deliberations. In many cases, the funder has little, if any, on-the-ground experience with the grantee, with the exception of pre-arranged site visits that are often rushed and not representative of the day-to-day life of a nonprofit operation. The beauty of being able to build relationships with your grantees, through proximity and concerted effort, is that you know in your bones, as well as with your eyes and ears, that the work is taking place effectively. If it isn't, then you roll up your sleeves to help problem-solve and engage in solutions. Intuition is a powerful leadership tool. It can be used in problem-solving, decision-making, and developing new insights. It is the thing that often made the difference between a satisfactory grantor-grantee relationship and a great one.

In another sense, we used our intuition as funders to answer the larger question: "How can we make the world a better place?" This is a complex puzzle, and is the question at the root of most nonprofit grantmaking. Very often, funders assign a rigorous and daunting set of questions and filters to potential grantees to find out if they are the right match for funding. By using a more intuitive approach, the Community Building Foundation used local knowledge, trust, and personal relationships to help our funding become the conduit for change. The vision of a river of funding that flowed to where it was needed, without the hindrances of complex applications and other time-consuming red tape, helped steer us toward a more relational approach. Harnessing intuition means using common sense. The grant making of the Community Building Foundation was not intended to be confidential or at arm's length. It was meant to be relational. This was how we knew that our shared values were making a difference in our community.

CHAPTER THIRTEEN

Envision Spokane:
The Community Bill of Rights Movement

By Kai Huschke

Kai was centrally involved in the first-in-the-nation Community Bill of Rights and Worker Bill of Rights, which both originated in Spokane. As an organizer with the Community Environmental Legal Defense Fund, Kai has supported community rights work around the world for the last thirteen years while continuing to call Spokane home.

The "community rights" movement aims to secure more legitimate power to local communities and governments, which have been historically vulnerable to the harmful actions of corporate interests. It has focused on empowering communities with the legal right to ban harmful activities that threaten human health, the environment, and local economies. It posits that a community, as a collective, can make governing decisions that are better for people and the planet, but that a community's power is too easily steamrolled by industry and special interest groups.

The growing community rights movement and its assertions of local community bill of rights laws owes a great debt to Spokane. In 2008, Spokane became the nation's first community—with assistance from the Community Environmental Legal Defense Fund (CELDF)—to draft a community bill of rights. Starting in Pennsylvania in 1995, other towns have worked with CELDF to change their municipal codes and charters and protect themselves from pending threats, but activists took the concept a step further in Spokane. They proposed a comprehensive Community Bill of Rights to redefine the city's home rule charter—akin to a local constitution for a city—with enforceable protections for neighborhoods, individuals, and the environment. The proposal of this Community Bill of Rights cracked open new possibilities and has been a spark for human, civil, and nature's rights within the community, the region, and across the nation.

It Started with Democracy School

Just as the civil rights movement had the Highlander Institute in Tennessee—attended by Rosa Parks and Martin Luther King Jr. —the emerging community rights movement has had Democracy School since 2005. Created and taught by CELDF, Democracy School has proven to be pivotal in the evolution of community rights nationally and in Spokane, one of the first communities to host the program. Over the years, Spokane has hosted nearly a dozen of these workshops.

The approach of Democracy School is to combine an approach similar to Howard Zinn's *A Peoples' History of the United States*—which includes education in civics, history, and law—with discussions on community organizing and the key tenets of what makes a successful social movement. The school teaches residents and activists how to reframe exhausting and often discouraging single-issue campaigns—such as opposing oil pipelines, gentrification, GMOs, attacks on worker rights, and pesticides—in a way that enables communities to confront corporate privilege. Attorney James Paulding explains the purpose of Democracy School this way: "The legislation passed at the state or federal level is often a result of successful lobbying efforts by industry and often a reaction to local-level ordinances and ensuing litigation. CELDF makes the argument that our current system of law prevents local environmental and economic sustainability. The Community Rights movement seeks to elevate the environmental, social, and economic rights of the community over the rights of armchair quarterbacking legislators, who are too frequently in the pockets of industry."

Over the course of the school, attendees learn that the Constitution is grounded in the protection of and advocacy for property, not rights, and that

Kai Huschke has spent over a decade supporting community rights work in Spokane

those who have property have access to the system and to justice, where others don't. A case is presented that governance, law, and ultimately the corporate form have been built on, and are guarded by, this property view of the world. People, communities, and nature are things—property—for a wealthy minority to largely control at will. As CELDF co-founder, Thomas Linzey, explains in an interview with Amy Goodman on *Democracy Now*: "Our environmental movement has always been based on nature as property. In other words, if you own ten acres of ground in the United States, [that ownership] carries with it the legal ability to destroy the ecosystems on that ten-acre piece of property. What is increasingly growing is a realization that for a real environmental movement to occur, that ecosystems must have legally enforceable rights of their own."

The presentations and discussions at Democracy School center around the system being intentionally designed to keep corporate elites in power, subvert the will of the people, and deny ecosystems inherent rights. The system is not broken and in need of fixing; rather, it is working exactly as intended. Throughout history, there have been clear movements—the American Revolution, abolition, and suffrage—towards greater rights, self-determination, and decentralization. But that work is not close to over. A more radical, systemic solution is needed to protect communities and to deeply change culture.

Envision Spokane co-founder Brad Read (left) along with Huschke (right) and organizers for Spokane's Worker Bill of Rights

Spokane — The Birthplace of the Community Bill of Rights

Democracy School came to Spokane when Jim Sheehan invited CELDF's Thomas Linzey to host Democracy Schools in Spokane. Until then, most of CELDF's community rights work had been assisting small, rural communities on the East Coast that were trying to halt toxic waste dumps, land applied sewage sludge, factory farms, and other kinds of exploitation. Jim and Thomas started discussing what it would look like to seed conversations about community rights in an urban environment. After attending Democracy School, Jim felt it was so important that he provided scholarship funds for other people to attend. It followed naturally that Democracy School hosted trainings at the Community Building Campus, which opened its meeting rooms to any nonprofit in the city. As momentum for community rights work swelled, meetings were held at the CBC so frequently that the campus became home base for community rights work in Spokane. Although the eventual Community Bill of Rights organizers went to community centers, neighborhoods, and labor halls, the CBC helped incubate the campaign by providing free and easily accessible space for early conversations, ongoing strategy sessions, and trainings.

It also followed naturally that Jim would become a committed patron of community rights work. Thanks to his career as a public defender, he saw that the system itself was broken and wanted to give people the space to imagine how they could effectively address systemic change on a local level. He made space for Spokane residents to go beyond challenging unjust laws in court and to consider changing the entire political system that birthed unjust laws in the first place. Jim is unique because he was willing to put his resources behind a radical grassroots campaign, and he invested in every iteration of the campaign because he knew that structural change cannot be accomplished through a single election. It must come from a movement mentality—one that redefines setbacks as wins and understands that culture shifts do not happen overnight.

What follows is a sometimes-uncomfortable account of Spokane's Community Bill of Rights, known as the Envision Spokane campaign, which both brought together and divided the local progressive community. Many activists and politicians, such as Breean Beggs (Chapter 7), were wary of Envision Spokane's more radical approach. And others like Mariah McKay (Chapter 15) felt the concept was sound but that our educational efforts were lacking. These differing points of view, all housed within the same progressive campus, show that systemic change campaigns are complex and largely difficult to understand in the moment. Like with any movement, what transpired with Envision Spokane wasn't perfect, but this Spokane-based advocacy for greater rights has inspired others in the state and across the country to take control of their well-being and have new conversations about the principles of our democracy.

Building a Movement

As the first round of Democracy Schools across Spokane wrapped up in the winter of 2007, seven people active on neighborhood, social justice, and environmental fronts gathered in a small living room in one of Spokane's poorest neighborhoods to talk about how to take back their community. As Mariah McKay (one of these original seven) discusses in Chapter 15, they came together to figure out how to implement what we were learning from Democracy School.

Seated on a puffy brown couch or the floor—drinks and snacks within arm's reach—the group, with guidance from the Community Environmental Legal Defense Fund, considered two questions: 1) What do we want in our community? and 2) Who decides? They had all been through Democracy School, and they asked themselves these questions because they understood that the tools, outlets, and options currently in place through conventional law and governance were not only inadequate, but unjust. They realized that conventional law and governance were the core of rapid environmental, social, and economic decline impacting Spokane and communities across the United States.

I got involved with the work around this time thanks to a connection through the Bioneers network which led me to Jim. He invited me on an in-depth tour of the renovations at the Saranac Building and told me about the conversations about community rights that were starting to take hold in Spokane through Democracy School. Little did I know that my life's trajectory would change so radically. I attended Democracy School, joined the effort to build out Envision Spokane, then started teaching Democracy School.

Our conversations focused on the growing disparity between the haves and the have-nots, a 2,000+ unit shortage of affordable low-income housing, local government favoring big box stores over local businesses, residents unable to determine the future of their neighborhoods, and a river on life support. These were just a few of the reasons why people saw the need to take greater control of the democratic process and to be more directly involved in making the laws that shaped their ability to make decisions in their communities.

When peeling the layers back of who really makes the critical decisions in a community, one finds oneself spinning into the distant past. A bundle of legal doctrines, including the federal Constitution, state preemption, Dillon's rule (privileging states' rights over local governments' rights), regulatory laws, and corporate constitutional rights (corporations are seen as "persons" under the law) function to squash community decision-making. The group, myself included, understood that stepping into this existing structure of law was untenable. Moving forward, we needed to restructure the system of law itself into one that values people, neighborhoods, workers, the local economy, and nature over state-protected corporate power.

From the original seven activists, the group quickly became thirty, representing twenty-four organizations—neighborhood associations, social service agencies, environmental organizations, and labor unions. Together, we formed a group called Envision Spokane and began exploring how to put the rights of residents, workers, neighborhoods, and nature above corporate interests. For five months, we met nearly weekly in the Community Building, discussing and drafting amendments to Spokane's home rule charter—the city's version of a constitution. In the fall of 2008, we released the nation's first Community Bill of Rights and petitioned to put it on the November 2009 ballot. It contained a robust statement of rights for a locally based economy, affordable and renewable energy, affordable preventive healthcare, affordable housing, a healthy environment, residents' ability to determine the future of their neighborhoods, constitutional protections in the workplace, and prevailing wage and work as apprentices on certain construction projects. In addition, it included an enforcement amendment subordinating corporate rights to community rights when they came into conflict.

Losing Is Part of Winning

Envision Spokane had set itself up to confront the powerbrokers of Spokane who pulled out all the stops to sway public opinion through email, letters, direct mail, meetings, mass media, and presentations on what the Community Bill of Rights contained and what it would do. In the first ballot campaign in 2009, the opposition raised nearly $500,000—85% coming from corporate lobbying organizations outside of Spokane—to persuade voters to vote no. Envision Spokane, on the other hand, elicited small-dollar donations from Spokane residents and organizations, along with a couple of generous donations. Working with a campaign budget of about $40,000 and lots of volunteer hours, Envision Spokane was strategic in its outreach to voters by distributing campaign flyers by hand, going door to door, organizing all-volunteer phone-banking sessions, and sending out targeted campaign mailers.

In conventional political terms, the defeat like the Community Bill of Rights suffered in 2009, when it lost by a three-to-one margin, marks an endpoint, not a waypoint. However, before the effort ever came before the voters, the core members of Envision Spokane understood that what we were embarking on was a journey that could take years and that a single election would not be enough to transform how government is structured.

A back-to-the-drawing-board approach was taken, and the group talked through what the next run of the Community Bill of Rights would look like. At the time of the vote on the Community Bill of Rights 2.0 in 2011, two national events had captured headlines. The first was the U.S. Supreme Court's decision in Citizens United v. Federal Election Commission, recognizing expanded rights for corporations to participate and ultimately influence elections. The second was the Occupy Wall Street movement that inspired copycat actions in hundreds of communities across the country, including Spokane, with powerful memes like: "We are the 99%." The winds had shifted, and Envision Spokane put forward the following abbreviated Community Bill of Rights:

Community Bill of Rights 2.0 (2011)

First. Neighborhood Residents Have The Right To Determine Major Development In Their Neighborhoods.

Neighborhood majorities shall have the right to approve all zoning changes proposed for their neighborhood involving major commercial, industrial, or residential development. Neighborhood majorities shall mean the majority of registered voters residing in an official city neighborhood who voted in the last general election. Proposed commercial or industrial development shall be deemed major if it exceeds ten thousand square feet, and proposed residential development shall be deemed major if it exceeds twenty units and its construction is not financed by governmental funds allocated for low-income housing.

It shall be the responsibility of the proposer of the zoning change to acquire the approval of the neighborhood majority, and the zoning change shall not be effective without it. Neighborhood majorities shall also have a right to reject major commercial, industrial, or residential development, which is incompatible with the provisions of the City's Comprehensive Plan or this Charter.

Approval of a zoning change or rejection of proposed development under this section shall become effective upon the submission of a petition to the City containing the valid signatures of neighborhood majorities approving the zoning change or rejecting the proposed development, in a petition generally conforming to the referendum provisions of the Spokane municipal code.

Second. The Right To A Healthy Spokane River And Aquifer.

The Spokane River, its tributaries, and the Spokane Valley-Rathdrum Prairie Aquifer possess inalienable rights to exist and flourish, which shall include the right to sustainable recharge, flows sufficient to protect native fish habitat, and clean water. All residents of Spokane possess fundamental and inalienable rights to sustainably access, use, consume, and preserve water drawn from natural cycles that provide water necessary to sustain life within the City. The City of

Spokane and any resident of the City or group of residents have standing to enforce and protect these rights.

Third. Employees Have The Right To Constitutional Protections In The Workplace.

Employees shall possess United States and Washington Bill of Rights' constitutional protections in every workplace within the City of Spokane, and workers in unionized workplaces shall possess the right to collective bargaining.

Fourth. Corporate Powers Shall Be Subordinate To People's Rights.

Corporations and other business entities which violate the rights secured by this Charter shall not be deemed to be "persons," nor possess any other legal rights, privileges, powers, or protections which would interfere with the enforcement of rights enumerated by this Charter.

A Near Win

On election night November 2011, I gathered with supporters of the Community Bill of Rights at the home of Jim Sheehan to watch the election results come in. It was a festive setting with plenty of food and drink, but nobody had any sense of what to expect. Although more organizations and individuals stepped forward to publicly support the Community Bill of Rights, the campaign resembled the first in that Envision Spokane was still outspent twenty to one. A group of people had gathered downstairs to watch the television announcements of results. I was upstairs with a smaller group huddled around a laptop computer on the Spokane County Elections website. At 8:30 p.m., the vote total on Proposition 1—Spokane Community Bill of Rights—came up on the screen. It was deadlocked at 50-50.

At first, a stunned silence overtook those staring at the screen. Less than a minute later, an eruption from downstairs filled the house as the group of television watchers received the news that the Community Bill of Rights was on the cusp of becoming law. When the dust settled in tallying all the votes, the Community Bill of Rights missed passing by 500 votes. In 2009, the Community Bill of Rights won zero precincts. In 2011, the Community Bill of Rights 2.0 won more precincts than it lost and received a clear message from the residents of Spokane: the grassroots campaign was gaining momentum, and our fight needed to continue.

Legal Challenges

Envision Spokane took the near win and ran with it. In short order, the same process was followed with review, discussion, drafting, filing, and eventually petitioning. The third-round language of the Community Bill of Rights looked nearly identical to the 2011 version. Envision Spokane had proved that the people of Spokane cared about the issues and understood the relationship between neighborhoods, the river, workers, and corporate power, and that they wanted to take deep action to course correct.

The signature gathering for the third Community Bill of Rights campaign kicked off in spring 2012. By the following spring, signatures had been submitted, and once again the Community Bill of Rights was on the ballot, this time for the November 2013 election. With extra months to work with, Envision Spokane hoped to build a strong and robust campaign to get the Community Bill of Rights adopted.

However, in June 2013, sixteen plaintiffs filed a lawsuit against Envision Spokane to block the citizen initiative from being voted on by the residents of Spokane. In September 2013, the judge appointed to the case made the decision to accept the argument that if the Community Bill of Rights were to be adopted, it would be beyond the city's power to enforce, so therefore the people must be denied their right to vote.

Envision Spokane appealed. Nearly a year and half later, the appeals court overturned the lower court, ruling that the Community Bill of Rights should go to a vote. A scramble then ensued as the corporate plaintiffs called in favors with statewide corporate and governmental associations to join them in persuading the Washington Supreme Court to take the case. The court agreed.

Arguments from both sides were heard in the fall of 2015. Essentially, the case pitted administrative procedure and beliefs that the courts could decide on legislative matters before legislation becomes actual law against the people's democratic rights to vote and to petition to change government.

In February 2016, the court ruled unanimously that local initiatives may be challenged before being voted on if it looks like the proposed laws might be in conflict with existing law. That decision not only killed the Spokane Community Bill of Rights, but it has put future local initiatives, no matter where in the state, on notice that unless what you are proposing is within the status quo, then the proposed law may never be voted on.

Elevating the Plight of the Working Class— The Spokane Worker Bill of Rights

With the Community Bill of Rights on ice, we turned our attention towards the ever-growing wealth gap and corporate control of workers, which represented a return to the earlier community rights conversations and to Spokane's pro-labor history. When community groups worked together to narrow the original Community Bill of Rights and create CBR 2.0, some of the important provisions for labor were shelved in order to create a more cohesive document that the group felt had the most resonance with the community and the best shot at being voted in. Our renewed focus on labor was also a nod to the early 20th century when Spokane was home to a strong chapter of the Industrial Workers of the World—also known as the Wobblies—who organized diverse laborers across resource extraction, agriculture, and other industries.

What would become the Worker Bill of Rights, which would be in front of voters in 2015, was heavily shaped by the economic and workplace inequity and injustice prevalent across the U.S.—stagnant wages since the 1970s, women and other marginalized peoples earning 77 cents on the dollar as compared to white men, employers wielding the power to fire workers for no cause (labeled in classic propaganda as "at-will" employment).

Spearheaded by Envision Spokane, a new coalition of citizens, labor union locals, churches, businesses, and social justice advocates worked together to draft and then advance a Worker Bill of Rights. In short, Spokane's Worker Bill of Rights would ensure people were paid adequately and justly and fired only if they were not doing their job. It also created the structure for a family wage, which would provide for steady wage increases over time, rather than a specific dollar increase. The rights-based proposal, like the Community Bill of Rights before it, was grounded in justice, equity, and sustainability.

Come summer of 2015 and for the fourth time, Envision Spokane qualified a citizens' initiative. The Spokane Worker Bill of Rights would be on the ballot, but not without another legal fight by those who didn't want the vote to happen, this time led by the sitting mayor of Spokane. However, unlike 2013, a different lower court judge made the decision that the Worker Bill of Rights should go before the voters. The judge's ruling made clear that the Spokane Worker Bill of Rights was a legislative matter for the people of Spokane, and until the Worker

Bill of Rights became law, the courts should not involve itself in the people's business. Despite endorsements from major unions in Spokane, thumbs up by national figures like Chris Hedges and Noam Chomsky, and international media coverage, the Spokane Worker Bill of Rights unfortunately did not pass in November 2015.

What Happened in Spokane
Didn't Stay in Spokane

Although the organization Envision Spokane has been dormant since 2016, Spokane has changed thanks to the campaign, and other communities have and will continue to push the boundaries towards justice, a more people-centered democracy, and a truly sustainable future.

It's challenging to draw direct lines between cause and effect, but I believe that putting the Community Bill of Rights in front of the people on several occasions helped aspects of the campaign to sprout in other ways. For example, the Responsible Bidder Ordinance was adopted by the City of Spokane in 2018 to protect workers and their interests during the bidding process over city contracts. Envision Spokane helped lay the groundwork for this ordinance by posing bigger questions about important labor protections in its campaigns. The city also adopted a broader neighborhood notification system for development. While this is not the same as securing greater decision-making power, now the whole neighborhood is notified of potential development projects instead of just the adjacent property owners.

Zooming out to impacts across the country tells a much more robust story. A year after Spokane's Community Bill of Rights lost at the ballot in 2009, the City of Pittsburgh adopted a Community Bill of Rights. That effort, though in a different city and addressing a different issue, owes its form and message to Spokane. And since Pittsburgh, dozens of other communities in other parts of the country have modeled their laws protecting the health, safety, and welfare of their communities after Spokane.

Within Washington, Spokane's efforts sparked people in Bellingham and Seattle to move away from conventional, in-the-box activism to one focused on the people seizing control of their right to self-determination and to use that power to challenge corporate projects aimed at overriding community will.

The collective efforts of Spokane, Seattle, and Bellingham spurred interest and efforts in other parts of the state such as Skagit County, Port Townsend, and Olympia. In the summer of 2012, the Spokane Declaration was adopted by community rights activists from five different Washington communities. The Declaration laid out that "our communities are under siege from corporations exploiting our communities for resource extraction and a variety of other uses harmful to us and the natural environment" and the need to "adopt local laws that recognize community rights for residents of Washington municipalities and the natural environment." That call to action helped launch the Washington Community Rights Network, an organization made up of and led by community members from different parts of the state.

Today, citizens in San Juan County, Snoqualmie County, and Pend Oreille County are also organizing on a community rights platform, owing their existence in part to what Envision Spokane started over ten years ago.

Washington's collective energy, even without a local community rights law being adopted in Washington State, helped provide a new path for communities in Oregon that are under assault from GMOs, the timber industry, and fossil fuels. Washington's local efforts function as a cornerstone for community rights in Oregon today, both at the local and state levels as community rights activists look to amend the state's constitution to recognize the right of local community self-government.

Despite the obstructionism and conventional losses, a bit of Spokane has been planted in other community rights efforts across the country, and some of those seeds are beginning to sprout. I feel lucky to continue with my organizing work and Democracy School training, helping other communities work through the same question as those original seven in Spokane: Who decides? The answer, which is gaining momentum across the country, is that when it comes to the health, safety, vitality, and sustainability of a community—of the people and the environment they are intrinsically connected to—then it is the community that must decide.

CHAPTER FOURTEEN

Wealth Management for Community Builders

By John Bjorkman

For almost forty years, John served as a CPA and financial adviser to hundreds of individuals, for-profit and nonprofit entities, their owners and key members. He now volunteers for a local charity, teaches part-time as an adjunct at a local university, and assists another longtime client with transitioning a family-owned business to the fourth generation.

In 2003, I became Jim Sheehan's adviser, and I have been involved in everything from purchasing new buildings to starting new legal entities to serving as the trustee on his children's trusts. It's been fascinating, chaotic, and unforgettable to work with Jim, his family, and his staff.

From the outset, Jim was noticeably different from our other clients. Rather than striving to maximize his wealth, his true focus is and always has been on making things better for the community—at times at the expense of his personal wealth. His philanthropy was not one more thing he did with his money; public benefit and the greater good were what his money was for. In the world of wealth management, I can tell you, this is rare.

Over the years, Jim's vision has constantly evolved. His willingness to change course and adapt to perceived needs within the community means that his financial strategy has been upended a number of times, leaving us to react and scramble rather than strategize and plan. However, witnessing how

Jim's unusual approach has transformed the lives of individuals and an entire neighborhood is one of the most memorable aspects of my career. In his eyes, community benefits are a better payback than accruing more wealth, and that's what has made him a truly stand-out character.

Now that I've left public accounting, I've had the chance to reflect on my journey with Jim and his family, and to gather some takeaways from our years of working together. It's important to know that these lessons extend to many people—not just those with considerable wealth. Everyone should be thinking about who they are, what matters most to them, and what they want their legacy on this planet to look like. Reflecting on this will help every individual make the best financial decisions for them, and for those who come after them.

1) Know Yourself and Your Core Values

It has been my experience that in order for me to be of any help to a client, it is important to learn as much as possible about them, their core values, and their long-term goals. The better these things can be understood and articulated, the more effective any planning or advice will be. That way, when they want to do something consequential like invest, make a big purchase, or donate to charity, you have context for effective decision-making and recommended courses of action.

Jim's his heart has always been to find a way to provide a helping hand to those less fortunate in our community, and those values have been unwavering, no matter how much money was in his bank account or who else is in the room. Jim's professional career started in the 1970s, when he began working with Dick Cease to help establish the Spokane Public Defender's office. Even then, Jim didn't take the prescribed route. The more common, financially advantageous, and arguably smarter move would have been to go into private practice as a litigator. But public defense was in line with his value system. Jim is unique because he's committed to the public good, but he is flexible and realistic about where living into these values will take him. The public defender's office gave him that realism and consistency.

Your values and goals shape every aspect of financial decision-making. With his newfound wealth, Jim followed his value system and established the Center for Justice, his first private foundation, a nonprofit public law firm focused on providing legal assistance to those who did not have the means to navigate our legal system.

Two years later, Jim formed his second charitable foundation so that he could support the community in ways outside of the Center for Justice framework. This nonprofit was called the Quiet Group. As the name suggests, Jim did not care about publicity; in fact, it was quite the opposite. This wasn't about Jim building a legacy for himself and his family name, but finding ways to build a better community for everyone. The name was eventually changed to the Community Building Foundation to better reflect not just the community of small nonprofits that became housed in the property owned by the foundation—the building now known as the Community Building—but also to reflect the long-term goal of helping build the community in general.

When you look at history, it might be argued that many philanthropists haven't been driven by altruism as much as narcissism—a charitable intent that's more about self-focused, grandiose ideas of leaving their permanent imprint on society. Their approach seems more like the pharaohs buying their way to eternal life than noble hearts hoping to leave a positive impact on society. They want something to be here after they are gone, to remember them by. They brand everything they touch with their image.

Of course, charitable giving can provide a legacy while also benefiting the greater good. But the concept of "good" must be deeper and more complex than an extension of a personal brand. The question cannot just be: "If I do this, how will it benefit me or my family personally?" Or, "How good of a tax break can I get?" The good must be rooted in one's core values, and the core values must be rooted in a cornerstone, like community.

2) Understand the Opportunity, Power, and Responsibility

Many people are intrigued by the concept of being wealthy, of having all the accoutrements that go along with wealth: new cars, boats, multiple homes, their own private foundation. But few people are equipped to navigate the complexities and moving pieces of managing large sums of money and assets. And while we might dream of winning the lottery, very few people have the training, the need, or the desire to learn how to properly manage millions of dollars to ensure they and their family are taken care of long term,or to protect themselves so they are not preyed upon or lose everything they have.

According to the National Endowment for Financial Education, 70% of

As Jim Sheehan's adviser, John Bjorkman has supported the CBC's growth since 2003

lottery winners end up broke, and a third go on to declare bankruptcy. Runaway spending, bad investments, greed, and bad advice can quickly deplete these holdings. Instant wealth can make it difficult for many people in relationships with their family, friends, and those in their immediate social or work circles who aren't so fortunate. Greed, envy, resentment, entitlement, and unrealistic expectations can all come into play.

Someone who works hard all their life to save a million dollars for retirement may not have the same appreciation for a windfall of that same amount received through an inheritance or winning the lottery. In fact, inheriting a substantial amount of money and winning the lottery can be a lot alike. In both scenarios, the change can be sudden, and the newly wealthy are unequipped for the burden that comes along with the blessing.

This was not the case for Jim, but then not many people's ethics and value systems are as grounded. He wasn't enamored by boats and airplanes or materialistic trappings. Jim looked at this sudden wealth from a hierarchy-of-need point of view. Once he realized he didn't have to work any longer and his family's basic needs were met, his thought process was something like: "Wow, I don't have to work anymore, and if I don't have to work, what else can I do? What are the needs in this community? What do we really need in this city?" Although it didn't take him long to retire from the public defender's office, in a way he never stopped working. Once his family was secure, he put the remainder of his sudden windfall to work in a different way.

Jim's trajectory and decision-making are interesting to me because others' understanding of their basic needs is a lot more opulent. I think this is driven by society. We live in a capitalistic democracy where economics influences everyone's view of what it means to be successful. Traditionally, and in the case of many of my clients, the more stuff you own, the more successful you are perceived to be.

How many homes, lake cabins, cars, motorhomes, and boats does a person really need? Knowing what is most important to you and your family—and again, keeping in touch with your core values—truly helps you navigate the responsibilities that come with wealth and significant amounts of money.

3) Consult a Diverse Team of Consultants and Advisers

Imagine you just won or inherited $10,000,000. What do you do with it? Put it in your checking account? Maybe the interest-bearing one at the credit union? Then what? You will probably need help with money management; legal documents such as wills, trusts, powers of attorney; help with taxes; the list goes on and on the more money and stuff you acquire. And you need to trust whoever you bring in to help with such matters.

In choosing advisers, it is critical to understand that in today's world people specialize, and no one person knows everything. You don't go to a heart specialist to have a knee replacement. To get the best advice and outcome, it's important to take a more holistic approach. Even though Jim was a licensed practicing attorney, his area of expertise was in litigation and public defense. He realized that he needed help from other attorneys and specialists to manage his windfall inheritance. He reached out to attorneys who specialized in the legalities and handling of wealth, who in turn recommended other specialists dealing with taxes and entity formation. Finally, he enlisted the help of investment advisers experienced in managing large sums of money. This formed his initial team.

Like having a general practitioner for a family physician to help coordinate specific health care, it is advisable to have a key trusted adviser (or as one my clients said, a "traffic controller") to help coordinate the activities and recommendations of your team of advisers—someone who knows and understands you, your family, and your goals and values. For Jim, that role has been a combination of his current investment adviser, Dave Martin, his attorneys, and me. Jim has been very fortunate over the years to have advisers who care about him and respect his core values and desire to build the community. When Jim consults one of us about buying a building or making a substantial contribution to another organization, we consult to make sure that the best possible outcome is achieved.

The questions go something like this: If Jim wants to fund a specific activity or organization other than one of his foundations, is it better to use funds from one of the foundations, write a check personally, loan them the money, or give them stock that is then sold by that organization? If buying a piece of property, why and what is the end use for that property? Which entity should own this property? Tax, legal, and organizational goals are all part of the decision matrix. Not taking Jim's goals into consideration or understanding his values and how everything is intertwined can create more problems and costs down the road. Recommendations and decisions need to be made in context.

For example, a lot of people are enticed by the idea of starting a private charity. While it is recommended to have substantial start-up capital, it actually doesn't take millions of dollars to start a private foundation. The fact is, it's fairly easy and relatively cheap to set up a private foundation or a charitable organization. There are companies that will cookie-cutter these things for you. But many people don't understand at the end of the day what setting up, funding, and managing a charitable entity means or what those commitments will really be. For the organization to succeed, you have to be committed to your cause long term. And even then, starting a nonprofit organization may not be the best option, which is why it's important to maintain flexibility. Jim's story is a case study for this.

4) Maintain Flexibility

When Jim formed the Center for Justice, that entity elected to be treated as a private operating foundation under the federal tax code. This allows a privately funded, nongovernmental entity to be treated as a nonprofit organization under a long list of very complex rules, as long as it acts like a public charity with all activities performed for public goodwill.

Any monies donated to the Center were treated like donations to any other public charity. Again, the rules are very complex, and these entities do not pay income taxes, but they do pay annual excise taxes on the value of their assets. They also pay penalties and additional taxes if they do not use or spend their monies in accordance with their stated mission. You can't just toss money into a private operating foundation and sit on it. It must be spent and used for the charitable purpose the entity was organized to do. This was a good decision, though, since the goal for the Center for Justice was to make it a publicly supported charitable organization for the long term.

Through the Community Building Foundation (formerly the Quiet Group), Jim used his own money to buy the properties that are now known as the Community Building and the Community Building Annex. Based upon his goals at that time—for example, allowing the Center for Justice and other nonprofits free or reduced rent—it was recommended that the property be donated to the Community Building Foundation, another separate distinct private foundation. The contribution of the ownership of the buildings created a charitable income tax deduction for Jim and put the oversight and management of the buildings under the new foundation. Additionally, monies Jim would spend personally to maintain and support the property would now be donated directly to the foundation to support the charitable endeavors of that entity and be tax-deductible by Jim as additional charitable contributions.

At that time, it was not envisioned that Jim would go on to acquire and revitalize several other buildings on that same block, or that part of his community-building philosophy would come to include commercial activities. It seemed like a private operating foundation would have the best long-term tax impact while also honoring Jim's goals and values. Jim has never been motivated by tax benefits but understands that any cash freed up from taxes can be used to support his charitable activities. If Jim could have articulated up front that his long-term plan was to develop and revitalize a large, rundown section of downtown Spokane for the benefit of the community at large, while helping other like-minded small nonprofits, the recommendation for the legal entities, structure, and property ownership would have been much easier. However, those were not defined goals at the outset. Jim's plan and the means to achieve his goals evolved as he did.

When Jim started looking at purchasing the old Hotel Saranac, which was to include a restaurant and pub, we knew we had to rethink how we were structuring Jim's legal entities. Jim was going to spend a substantial amount of money not just purchasing the properties, but also rehabilitating the buildings. Cash was needed to help launch the for-profit startup businesses that would be occupying the newly acquired properties. From a tax point of view, pouring money into a private foundation can be beneficial for individuals who have significant amounts of taxable income. However, contributions to such entities are subject to significant limitations under the tax code, which decrease or, as in Jim's case, can disallow any tax-saving benefits. Further complicating matters is that, in general, qualified charitable entities cannot own or operate for-profit businesses that are outside of the immediate services or charter of that nonprofit organization. For a charitable entity, operating or owning such activities creates significant adverse income tax issues at a minimum, and in the worst case, dissolves the charitable entity. Jim's vision included such for-profit activities.

If Jim was going to invest large sums of his own money into buying and rehabilitating commercial properties while getting some for-profit businesses up and running, then the best structure for owning, investing in, and managing those activities would not be inside of a charitable entity like one of the foundations, but through a for-profit entity. The Saranac LLC, a for-profit taxable entity, was structured and tasked as the main vehicle to own and operate those properties and their related activities. Managing the buildings out of an LLC instead of a foundation removes the possibility for self-dealing and allows for flexibility in case he decided to buy or sell in the future. Jim's investment into those buildings, surrounding real estate, and businesses would hopefully increase his net worth in the long run while supporting several nonprofits and rebuilding that entire section of Spokane and the surrounding community. Everyone would benefit, not just Jim.

The setup, funding, and management of these two foundations has been a constant balancing act involving Jim and his whole team of advisers. It could not have been accomplished without the specific talents of everyone involved, and definitely not without understanding Jim's core values and what he wanted to accomplish in the community. The current structure of entities allows Jim— and now his family—future flexibility as the immediate needs and opportunities change, and as Spokane changes.

5) Accept That the Only Constant Is Change

As noted above, private foundations are complex animals, as you are required by law to act in the interests of the public good while overseeing and using your own money and assets to do so. The penalties for noncompliance are extreme, and the annual reporting and accounting are incredibly involved. The entity and all its activities are subject to the scrutiny of the IRS, and also whatever state you are operating in. These private foundations are much easier to get into than they are to get out of. Once money and assets go into the charitable entity, those assets are exempt from estate tax, their contribution gives you an income tax deduction, and you also receive some tax benefits from states and cities.

But once you tire of it, or no one is there to continue organizational leadership, you can't just dissolve that entity, grab whatever assets remain, and go on your way. The assets of that entity have to go to another qualified charitable entity. That money is locked in for the public benefit in perpetuity.

Such was the case for the Center for Justice. At one point in time, the entity was able to not only become self-sustaining but achieve the necessary public support through donations and performing the necessary services to become a bona fide, public, 501c3 charity. However, that was an extremely difficult struggle to maintain, as it is with many small nonprofits. In 2020, the Center for Justice legal entity was dissolved, and its assets and programs, like Spokane Riverkeeper, were disbursed to other qualified 501(c)(3) charitable organizations in the community.

It doesn't matter if you are a nonprofit or for-profit business; it's important to remember that things can and will change. I suspect that Jim probably knew deep down where he wanted to go from the outset, but he didn't know exactly how it would happen. When he acquired that first building, I don't believe he knew that he was going to purchase six buildings on a single block, but he knew he wanted to help build the community in downtown Spokane. The better you can articulate goals and plans, the easier it is to land upon the right structure and bring the right people into your vision—assets that will serve you when you need to adapt to changes that are outside of your control, and changes you make to enhance and better achieve your goals.

The full, long-range impact of Jim's endeavors on the community of Spokane are still in progress and now in the capable hands of his family and key individuals who support Jim's efforts. Things will keep changing, and how the Community Building Foundation and Saranac LLC evolve to influence that change is yet to be determined. Jim, Katy, and Joe are still working on that, and they are not the only members of the next generation who are trying to do things differently.

At this time, an unprecedented transfer of trillions of dollars of wealth has begun, from the Baby Boomer generation to their successors. Estimates suggest that fifteen to fifty trillion dollars will change hands in the next twenty years. Jim was the immediate beneficiary of the start of this transfer, twenty years ago, and now his family—and more importantly, the greater Spokane community—stand to benefit from this legacy and all the lessons learned along the way.

CHAPTER FIFTEEN

Raised by Community

By Mariah McKay

Although Mariah found her stride as a leader at the CBC, her influence reaches far beyond. She is building Spokane's first cohousing community and is the founder of the Spokane Independent Metro Business Alliance.

In high school, my home was located outside the city limits in a conservative Christian area in north Spokane near Whitworth University. I butted heads with the public school system early and often. I was a very bored, supposedly advanced honors student who was ostracized for being a creative child with a hyperactive imagination. This feeling of not belonging continued through middle and high school, and I signed up for every possible activity to keep myself from disengaging. The lack of autonomy given to students felt like jail. I was involved in an environmental science club, which went defunct from lack of participation; I was involved in an equity and diversity club, which fell apart after I graduated. I was always on this marginal, ragged edge of involvement with the formal system. I've felt a deep need to belong and to be accepted, and to extend that relationship to everyone else in the community, regardless of their affiliations and identities.

Somehow, through the Unitarian Church I got connected with the Peace and Justice Action League of Spokane (PJALS), which had an office in the Community Building. At the time, they had a Youth for Social and Political

Change group, which was drastically different from the other church-affiliated youth groups my neighbors attended. This meeting was full of punky, anarchist kids from Lewis and Clark High School making political signs in the lobby of the Community Building such as "Stop War for Profit and Plunder." This was about 1999, and I remember getting the tour and walking up the stairs to KYRS—it felt right.

The newly remodeled windows framed in wood let in lots of natural light, and I felt the quality of the materials used in the remodel. Everything was built on a human scale. It was a place for sharing, a place where each different organization had its nook in a labyrinthine layout that seemed to keep going and going. It felt too good to be true, but there it was. I remember feeling like maybe my neighborhood was alienating, depressing, and didn't make any sense, but somewhere in this city there was a compassionate, open-door space where exciting things were happening. However, as a minor I couldn't easily access the CBC. I was just getting a driver's license, and public transportation to the north side was limited at the time. I was also oversubscribing to school activities just to cross the graduation finish line, which further isolated me, ironically, from being able to get involved in cultural and social activities downtown. So, while I knew about the energy and vibrancy emerging on that block on Main Avenue, it would be several more years until I plugged in and had a chance to fully connect.

I didn't get to start in earnest at the Community Building until I came back from college. I had graduated from Reed College with a degree in biochemistry and molecular biology, and I wanted to be a pharmaceutical sales rep to help pay for law school, where I thought I wanted to learn to practice biotech patent law. But when I returned to Spokane to get my bearings, there was an industry-wide hiring freeze. Fortunately, my mother had relocated from the north side to the Peaceful Valley neighborhood, which is adjacent to downtown. I met a neighbor who was a DJ at KYRS. He said the station was hiring AmeriCorps positions, and so I interviewed and was hired on as a volunteer coordinator.

Through my involvement at the radio station, I gained an appreciation for the way Spokane had all the raw ingredients of a truly great American city: It had diverse communities and people from different ethnic and racial backgrounds; it had subcultural groups like those found at the radio station—a rockabilly scene and a noise punk scene; it had long-standing communities of artists and thinkers and doers who had persevered without any institutional support for their craft.

Mariah McKay has figuratively and literally built community in the Spokane region

These factors created a palpable sense of authenticity. People who flip houses look at a structure and say, it has good bones. I started to feel that way about Spokane when walking from Peaceful Valley along Main Avenue to the Community Building every day. That was my commute for a whole summer, and that is when I began a decade-long process of deprograming. I started to consider a different paradigm for success and to develop a deeper sense of mission alignment. The indoctrination that I needed to be a certain kind of person and go a certain kind of direction slowly melted away. It took me years to find meaningful work, feel my power, and learn how to contribute in an integral, local community, but that phase of life nurtured a new vision for my city.

I would drive my brother's beat-up ambulance out to Medical Lake to set up the radio station's booth at a delightful bluegrass festival, join a mob of cyclists for a bike ride to dive bars across the city after work, and then stay up until 1 a.m. blogging for the *Spovangelist*, trying to make sense of all the unexpected and novel encounters I would share with fellow Spokanites throughout the day. Spokane is a place that seems to defy the odds against it. It forces you to stop and ask, "What are we all really doing here together?" I started to wonder why every block couldn't be like the Community Building block. I wondered, why are all these talented, young, creative professional types flocking to Portland when there were so many opportunities here in Spokane to exert leadership and create the kind of world we want to live in?

I didn't initially choose to stay in Spokane, but I kept finding reasons to stay, nonetheless. Because of my experience at the radio station, I was recruited to participate in Democracy School (Chapter 13). Democracy School is a two-and-a-half-day training that suggests the need for recognizing and preserving community rights, not just individual or corporate rights. This framework offered an answer to why our city and our community wasn't reaching the potential it seemed to have. It showed me early on the need for structural change. The Community Building Foundation bankrolled the program because of its importance to society.

As part of Democracy School, we broke into a neighborhood cluster, labor cluster, and community groups cluster. The idea was to create caucuses of different types of community leaders who could workshop with each other to define their struggles and needs. We then came together to compare notes across experiences to generate consensus upon a proposed "Community Bill of Rights," which we workshopped further with the public in Town Hall meetings. I was in my early twenties and ended up being in charge of the community groups cluster. Our charge was to answer the question, "What do our communities truly want and need?" not just, "What do we think we can get?" and then to think about what kind of legal rights could help us create that better world. I recruited organizational leaders to participate, scheduled meetings, took notes, and participated in discussions.

Over the year of dialogue hosted at the Saranac Building, we got to know all the groups around the table, hear concerns, compare notes, and develop a shared analysis around why we weren't achieving change at a rate that was proportional to the challenges we faced. Envision Spokane (Chapter 13) grew out of the Democracy School trainings as an attempt to implement our learning in our own city. People had gone through Democracy School, and we had that base to draw from as we explored why current advocacy work was falling short of the change we needed to effect on this planet. That was a special opportunity for a young thinker to be intimately involved in. I was given a chance to meaningfully address root causes of the challenges I saw in my community. I got to participate in a well-resourced initiative where my voice and critical thinking skills were taken seriously. Too few people of any age in our society have the fortune of participating in a civic effort like that.

We developed a platform for what a Community Bill of Rights would look like in Spokane. We did six town halls around the city. We distributed sixty thousand copies of the document, incorporated seven hundred points of feedback, and whittled it down to eight rights that we felt were foundational to succeed as a region as we, the community, defined it: creating a more sustainable society with a higher quality of life for community members. Then the next step was to take it to the ballot.

I felt strongly that this step was premature. I thought more public education was needed to win public support before pursuing a municipal ballot measure. I declined to participate in the campaign even though I supported the principles of the measure. I knew it wasn't going to be a winning electoral strategy at the point, but people were impatient to take action. They got about 25% of the vote the first year. They were outspent drastically. It was pretty brutal. For anyone paying attention—anyone who had the luxury, time, privilege, and space to pay attention—it showed who is who in protecting corporate power and access to wealth accumulation.

Observing the life and death of a meaningful, paradigm-shifting campaign was an instructive experience for me as an organizer and young changemaker. This is just one way in which my professional experiences have been shaped by the Community Building Campus. It's hard for me to reflect fully on the gaping power imbalances in our community, and it's even harder to directly confront what we're up against. But what's even more painful than the difficulty of the work is to contemplate what we face without this kind of space to hold us together in the fight. It is the difference between being a defenseless romantic in a gladiator's arena, as compared to being a well-equipped romantic who is surrounded by friends in a genuinely traumatized world. With the community that has grown around the organizations in the CBC, we have a fighting chance to create a more compassionate culture and humane society. That gives us just enough hope to keep trying no matter the daunting odds.

Through the Community Bill of Rights project, I met Dan Baumgarten, the executive director of Community Minded Enterprises (CME). After the biotech company I was working for laid off a third of its personnel due to cash flow issues, Dan offered me a job because he had been impressed with my leadership and critical thinking skills. I had never been offered that kind of validation or mentorship as a young person before. Neither of my parents were in this work, nor any of my friends or other family members at the time. It was a tough environment because I was hired to do grant writing, and a few months later the recession of 2008 took place. I was a science major with little formal writing background and no nonprofit experience writing grants in the worst economy in one hundred years. This experience exposed me to the irresponsibility of funds being dangled out there and then disappearing overnight. I saw important state grant programs get eliminated right when the public need was the greatest. All this was affecting me personally as CME was forced to keep cutting my hours.

I took on a second job with Anne Martin and the Win/Win Network in the Saranac Building, which became Greater Spokane Progress. My project, called NextUp Spokane, was a ten-hour-a-week youth civic engagement initiative. It was under-resourced and ill-fated and got defunded eventually, but this education in the precarious nature of funding for community projects influenced my trajectory in an important way. It showed me the need for locally funded, self-sustaining work to achieve long-term change.

After taking a third job working on the Community Building's website, I received an invitation to work for Senate Majority Leader Lisa Brown in Olympia; it was an offer I couldn't refuse. As a legislative aide, I got to hear from a broad constituency of people in Spokane. Because of the regressive and counter-cyclical way in which Washington State collects revenue, many life-saving programs had run out of funds in the wake of the recession, and massive budget cuts were taking place with serious consequences for peoples' lives. Without a strong political majority and the will to enact needed tax reform, our sales-tax-heavy system without a capital gains or income tax was leaving the legislature to make many penny-wise and pound-foolish decisions.

There was a lack of public education and misinformation about taxes, and little understanding of what money goes where. At the time, there was no organization in Spokane to engage people in a sustained state-wide fight to reform our revenue system to collect the resources that were needed. Organizations like PJALS would show up reliably for lobby days, but they didn't have the resources to travel frequently and lobby for comprehensive revenue reform. When I saw one hundred grassroots activists take over the capitol for a night and provide the impetus for lawmakers to finally step forward to propose various tax loophole closure bills to put money where it was needed most, I applied to become a community organizer with Washington CAN. I worked statewide from Olympia for two years and then eagerly relocated to Spokane. I opened an office in PJALS' spare room in the Community Building. It was the fulfillment of a dream that I could come back home to help address unmet needs I saw while working here and in the capitol. I followed one logical step to the next, and it led me all the way back to the Community Building where I had started.

These experiences, combined with three years at the Spokane Regional Health District, informed my next stage of investment in the Spokane community: a cohousing neighborhood called Haystack Heights and the Spokane Independent Metro Business Alliance (SIMBA). Through cohousing, we are doing in a residential setting what the CBC has done in a commercial setting for the social benefit sector. Through SIMBA, we are organizing independent and values-driven businesses and conscientious consumers to build a more equitable and resilient local economy. Much of our work involves educating people about the need for "triple bottom line" economics. We need to develop systems that reward businesses for accounting fully for their environmental and social impacts, as well as their profit potentials. Some call this the "Three Ps" of people, profit, and the planet. Others add in a fourth "P" for policy, to account for how fairly companies are governed.

The need for a business organization like this first came up when I was working on Sustainable September at Community-Minded Enterprises. Through the month-long festival's "green business" track, local business leaders brought Michelle Long to speak about the Business Alliance for Local Living Economies. I had already done some business organizing through Washington CAN and the Main Street Alliance around health care and immigration reform. We held press conferences, published op-eds, and appeared in reports on issues statewide. I had even traveled with small business owners to D.C. to take direct action on the issue of retirement security. I knew my audience, I had built teams before, and I found a funding opportunity to give me a runway to build up locally renewable membership contributions. I was able to build on my background from CME in grant writing and organizing fundraising events. I've been fortunate to get to participate in this landscape and observe how other organizations operate. This community has raised me and has informed every ounce of what I do today.

When I tell people about my work in Spokane, universally the response is, *wow, I wish I had that sense of commitment; I wish I had that sense of rootedness, purpose, and place.* Many people are still struggling to find a place on this earth where they feel they can belong and invest in meaningful relationships. They may move from city to city, job to job, relationship to relationship, and they still feel like they haven't found it. I think most young people have this fantasy of creating something like what we have here in Spokane, and here we are, thriving in our dusty little city! I understand this uniqueness as a treasure born of scarcity.

I've learned to appreciate that kind of creative dynamic. You have to abuse the grapes a little to get them to taste their sweetest. You have to repeatedly cut back the vine and not water it too much. It's similar here; Spokane has its fair share of hardships that resilient people have had to overcome. We need to shift away from saying we're marginal or we're on the edges and instead say, "This is exactly the kind of environment in which innovation takes place, and that's why we are worth investing in!" We are a mix of ideals in a very real place.

Through SIMBA, we are working to make sure Spokane continues to be this kind of dynamic, relational place, while rectifying inequities that have been constructed along lines of race and other marginalized identities. In addition to my own intergenerational, race, and class privileges, I'm concerned that the opportunities I had as a young professional are no longer available to a young person graduating from college today, just ten years later. Rents are higher and wages haven't increased. By combining our savings and incomes, my husband and I were able to buy our first house within walking distance of downtown. We rented out every room and made it affordable, but I don't think two young people in our positions could buy that house today. It's a clear example of how there's something fundamentally broken about the way wealth is accumulating and resources are distributed in our society.

As we approach peak resources, we're not going to be able to go back and rebuild all the places where people live. At some point, we're going to have to make do with the hand we're dealt, and we're in for a long, rough road. We are not setting ourselves up for stability. As a daughter of a cynical survivalist, my motto is, "prepare for the worst and hope for the best." But having contemplated the worst, I've spent a lot of time thinking about dire scenarios. Everything cannot go on as it always has so far in my lifetime. The key is to break out of this collective delusion and fight for a more equitable and sustainable future with a diminishing opportunity to get there while minimizing human suffering.

It's critical to recognize that growth is getting more and more expensive, that we can't grow forever, and that growth is not limitless. Our entire economic system is based on a faulty growth model, and it needs to be reengineered. What needs to happen now is for young people who share this perspective to band together and storm the halls of power and take over. We can't just be on our little block anymore. We have to send ambassadors to disrupt the conversations at powerful tables. I try to do this where I can through SIMBA and cohousing and in other venues, but it takes all of us.

CHAPTER SIXTEEN

Arts, Entertainment & Social Change

By Joe Sheehan

Joe is the manager of the Magic Lantern, a movie theater in the Saranac Building that is owned and operated by the Saranac LLC. He is Jim Sheehan's son and has occupied many different roles with multiple organizations on the Community Building Campus over the years, from construction crew to volunteer to property management to board member.

Watching movies at home was a revelation in the early 1980s, when VCRs became more ubiquitously available and you could pop down to the video store and rent the latest flick or an old classic. Some people thought this trend would drive movie theaters out of business, but the big theater complexes managed to hang on. Even now, with our huge selection of online streaming services and high-definition home TV screens—and in spite of seemingly endless trailers and advertisements preceding showtime—people still want to recline in giant red Naugahyde seats and watch newly released blockbusters while eating buckets of overpriced popcorn and guzzling soda from huge waxy cups. It is definitely one way to watch a movie, and it's an experience that we get to enjoy in chain multiplex theaters all across America. I like going to see movies this way as much as the next guy.

The Magic Lantern Theatre's sign along Main Avenue

I have the opportunity to view movies in a completely different way here in Spokane. Not only that, I get to manage the theater that shows them. I get to do this because my father is the founder of the Community Building Campus and its ethic. And because, thankfully, I am well-suited for the job.

The Magic Lantern is a small, independent, arthouse theater with two screens tucked inside the cozy brick walls at the back of the Saranac Building. There is an old-fashioned marquee out front on Main Avenue, but if you didn't know we were here, you could miss us entirely. Maybe not the savviest business move, but it does give us a quaint and laid-back feel that is comfortable and inviting, which is what we're all about. The aroma of freshly popped popcorn certainly helps—that, and it's not unusual for theater staff to be on a first-name basis with patrons. Off the lobby, heavy velvet curtains frame each theater entrance. The "big" theater seats 102. The small theater seats 33.

You are probably familiar with the term "arthouse theater" but also might be wondering what it is, exactly. Arthouse films are artistic works that are often experimental in nature. They champion a filmmaker's artistic vision over profit or pure entertainment, and arthouse theatres champion those films.

Or at least that is what we are going for. We have always wanted the theater to be inviting, but also a place to be entertained and even challenged. Terms like "serious artistic work" could lead to a philosophical debate over the definition of good art, or an exploration of what art is. But that is not a conversation that I find interesting to read or write about. What I do want to explore is what happens when art is present, as it has been since we opened the Community Building in 2001.

But this story starts before the launch of the Community Building Campus because the Magic Lantern has a long history in Spokane. It opened in the early '70s in a very small space up a narrow staircase above a restaurant and next to a bookstore and train tracks. I'm told you could feel the trains rumbling by during the shows. They showed mostly foreign films that would not have come to Spokane otherwise. I was not around back then, but this was before Spokane hosted the 1974 World's Fair, which completely changed the downtown from a central railway station into Riverfront Park.

Growing up in Spokane, I did not think of it as a culturally vibrant place. But we did have an independent movie theater. I do not remember downtown Spokane having much of nightlife, but maybe that is not entirely a fair assessment since I was a child and was told to be home from the park by dark. Still, even at seventeen or eighteen, when I could explore on my own a bit more, Spokane did not look promising to me. It was around that time in the late '90s that the Magic Lantern closed its doors after a nearly thirty-year run. I left Spokane for college and thought, "I will never live here again." Not because the Magic Lantern closed its doors, obviously, but because Spokane was the kind of city that had a few hundred thousand people and no independent movie theater! I was hardly the only person I knew that grew up here and left thinking, well, that's that. It seemed that Spokane was losing many of its best and brightest youths to other places. It was missing a generation of young leaders who wanted to invest their lives and lay down their own roots in their hometown.

I left in 2001 and returned in 2008, for many reasons. Among them, I had taken much of what Spokane offers for granted. It is, of course, common for young people to have conflicted relationships with the places they grew up. I could list so many things that I love about this place now—and things that were here all along. But I still need to admit that much of the reason I returned is that Spokane was changing. Perhaps it was underway long before I recognized it, but on my return visits for holidays I really became taken with the block that my father had a hand in redeveloping. Exciting things were happening, and you could see it.

In September 2007, I came back to Spokane to attend and support my father during the grand opening of the Saranac Building, his most ambitious project yet. Part of that ambition was relaunching the Magic Lantern, which had been dormant for years. Attempts had been made to find new locations but ultimately never manifested until the Saranac development took shape. A deal was struck, and the theater was going into the project—literally, the theater had to be carved into the building. Floors had to be opened and reframed to fit the inclined, theater-style seating. Walls had to be soundproofed. Air ducts had to be installed to cool down the projection rooms. Most of the building renovation involved converting living space into office space. Designs were often made with specific tenants' needs in mind, but those spaces could be rented again without much hassle if those tenants moved on. In this regard, the theater was a big commitment. If the theater failed, it would be hard and expensive to repurpose the space without a complete overhaul. This made the decision to invest in the theater a long-term commitment to its success.

The grand re-opening of the Magic Lantern was the finale of an all-day affair celebrating the Saranac Building's opening. My father glad-handed while I stood there and got introduced to many people. When it was time to start the show, we were exhausted and decided to skip the movie for a much-deserved dinner and rounds of beer. In traditional Magic Lantern fashion, they showed the soon-to-be Oscar-winning French film and Edith Piaf biopic, *Le Vie en Rose*. It sold out. There was so much excitement that Spokane's arthouse theater had returned. I moved back to Spokane a year later.

Until the COVID-19 shutdown, the Magic Lantern was experiencing the strongest run of success that I have witnessed since its move into the Saranac Building. I cannot speak to the business of the previous location, but considering its size and our slightly larger space, I would like to claim the healthiest run ever.

What made it successful in its current iteration? First and foremost, it is the quality of movies we show. My colleague and program director, Jonathan Abrameon, has been programming for the Magic Lantern for many years. He worked for the previous owner before they closed their doors in August of 2016. The decision to hire him led to a pretty seamless transition when the Saranac LLC took over operations in December of 2016 after the previous owner retired. Jonathan has always brought a wide array of genres, and the theater receives a lot of praise for his selections. In 2020, *The Inlander* named the Magic Lantern as "the best place in Spokane to expand your artistic horizons." Our concession sales have consistently increased since we took over operations, as well. I chalk this up to being the only first-run theater in town that serves beer and wine, and we have a small popcorn machine which requires us to make fresh popcorn constantly.

A major factor contributing to our success has been the implementation of community events and rentals. The Magic Lantern has always done these types of events but perhaps never quite realized the full potential of this aspect of the business. It was the hope when the theater opened in the Saranac Building that community events would become a regular occurrence and a part of the business model. This is where I came in. When the Saranac decided to take over operations of the theater, we hired Jonathan knowing what we were going to get: a program director who knew our audience and an in-house booking agent who could be given autonomy over the films he wanted to screen. Jonathan books the movies, handles all the shipping details, builds the shows on our software, and makes the film schedule—all while running the front of the theater most days. It is a full-time position. He needed help to expand the operating capacity of the theater and handle more bookings. The theater also needed more people to handle community outreach, negotiate rentals, and relieve Jonathan of always running the front of the theater. The Magic Lantern reopened under Saranac management in December of 2016, and I joined in February of 2017. At the time, we weren't open every day because we couldn't justify the doors being open. We simply didn't have the numbers. Within a few months, that changed.

It took time, but over the next couple years we made big strides in expanding our capacity. I was the contact person for handling most of our rental requests. Jonathan had existing relationships and maintained many of them, including with the Spokane International Film Festival, or SpIFF. The festival is typically our busiest week of the year and an exciting part of Spokane's art scene. It is hugely beneficial for us to confidently rely on business coming from established events. I spent about a year negotiating every rental on a case-by-case basis. I was trying to ensure that events were happening in our space no matter what. As the requests became more frequent, I had the ability to streamline that process a bit more, and what really made a difference was repeat customers.

We have always offered nonprofits a significant discount because we want to promote the progressive work happening in our community. This is how we can participate in the greater mission of the campus. Our location inside the Saranac Building and next to the Community Building means that we are surrounded by nonprofits, organizations filled with some of the most ambitious, hard-working people I have come across. They are activists who are working to change culture for the betterment of our society and our environment. They have grand ideas of the changes that need to be made. They have raised funds, built campaigns, organized rallies and protests, and participated in movements to change culture. The Magic Lantern has become a tool for many of these people and organizations. We are an excellent venue for promoting the messages that these organizations work so hard to bring to the public. We frequently work with our neighbors, including 350 Spokane (the local 350.org affiliate), KYRS Thin Air Radio, The Lands Council, Blueprints for Learning, Save Our Wild Salmon, Peace and Justice Action League of Spokane, and more. And these are just our neighbors.

Of this whole development project, the Magic Lantern is one of the touchpoints that reaches well beyond the occasionally isolated echo chamber of the progressive movement. Other organizations and businesses certainly have reach, but a movie theater has a uniquely broad appeal. I see this on a weekly, if not daily, basis.

Still, I think we appeal mostly to like-minded people and organizations, and some of our most fruitful relationships have come from the Social Justice Film Festival, The Alliance for Media Arts and Culture, and *The Black Lens*. The Social Justice Film Festival comes out of Seattle, and we have hosted a somewhat truncated version of their festival in Spokane the last couple of years. It has taken place over a single weekend, but the content was so good that some local folks used it to start a Meaningful Movies series with us. Once a month, they screen a film and host a discussion afterwards.

The Alliance started a documentary series, which is in its third season. Alliance director Wendy Levy hosts each screening and often organizes a panel discussion or performance of some kind related to each documentary's subject matter. Some of last season's wide-ranging films and subjects included *Dreamcatcher* (sex trade and abuse and exploitation), *Always in Season* (the descendants of victims and perpetrators of lynching), *Miss Sharon Jones!* (a singer's diagnosis and recovery from pancreatic cancer), and *One Child Nation* (China's population growth policies).

Sandy Williams, who runs *The Black Lens*, has hosted numerous fundraisers for her independent newspaper and the newly founded Carl Maxey Center. She routinely sells out the theater. People show up for Sandy, so we inform her whenever we think there is a movie coming that might offer an opportunity for her to host a discussion and raise some money for her organizations. Sandy has hosted a screening for *I Am Not Your Negro*, a James Baldwin documentary. This happened to be our first big event after the Saranac took over operations, and it sold out so fast that we had to schedule another screening that also sold out. She has also hosted for *Get Out*, *BlacKkKlansman*, and *Amazing Grace*, an Aretha Franklin concert documentary.

This is one of the things that makes the Magic Lantern such a special and unique place even among independent, community, arthouse theaters. Our community itself is largely responsible for programming. We may only organize six to ten events or rentals in a month, but they are frequently our busiest and most dynamic nights. And through these events over the last few years, we have built a reputation as a good host and expanded our reach even more. As the contact person for community events and rentals, I don't have to come up with many original programming ideas myself. I am approached by others with plans and ideas and funding. Then it becomes my job to best accommodate those factors so that everyone can enjoy a well-run event.

Accommodating rentals and events used to be a challenging proposition for us at times. Early on, Jonathan and I were operating a two-screen theater with one digital projector, and it severely limited our options. We were not able to show much in our small theater since we were limited to DVD and Blu-rays as formatting options. Distributors want their movies shown in high-quality formats and will refuse to send copies of their movies if a theater's specifications are not up to a certain standard. In October 2017, we installed a second digital projector in our small theater, and it changed so much of how we did business by giving us the freedom to schedule events without sacrificing our first-run films for the public.

Digital projection is a huge challenge for many small-time movie theaters. Around 2013, nearly all movie theaters were required to upgrade to digital projectors. They were being forced to by the distributors, who were shifting their format. Film reels were no longer being shipped around the country for distribution. Old film projectors were obsolete. The challenge was in coming up with the funds for such an upgrade. Any theater with multiple screens was looking at substantially more to invest so they might keep up. Our theater took four years and a change in ownership before we had both theaters outfitted with the necessary equipment. Many small theater operations died all over the country during this time. The large corporate theaters, which face their own challenges, had a much easier time spending the thousands of dollars to upgrade their multiplexes because they could count on the next blockbuster for instant cash flow. We did not have that luxury.

Joe Sheehan, manager of the Magic Lantern

Almost all our rentals are in our large theater and during prime evening hours, but having the small theater outfitted for digital formatting allowed us to continue to show our most popular movies at desirable showtimes. Additionally, it meant we could add more shows each day, which allowed us to book more movies, which gave us a greater marketing presence, as we had more to introduce week in and week out. We became more efficient in our staffing as well. The old film projectors essentially required a full-time position because you needed to switch reels and thread them through the projector for each individual picture. And when something went wrong with the films, which occurred much more frequently on those old projectors, someone had to be there to fix it. Meanwhile, someone else needs to handle concessions, ticket sales, cleanup, etc. Now, with the digital projectors, movies can be built and programmed in advance, and everything on that side operates automatically. During our slower times, we can operate the theater with a single employee acting as your ticket attendant, bartender, concessions salesperson, custodian, and projectionist all in one.

Even with the projector upgrade, we face many challenges running a small business. As I sit here, I am under a stay-at-home order due to COVID-19, and I have been reading up on the movie industry and its current state of flux. Theaters are closed. Streaming services have a virtual monopoly on the new movie experience. Simultaneously, there are hardly any new movies coming out, other than the ones already slated to open on streaming services. The big productions are pushing back their release dates so that they have a chance to recoup their enormous investments. They must cater to the multiplex theater experience because they need their movies to be shown as many times in a day as possible, for as many weeks as possible.

We are technically competing with other content providers, like the multiplexes and streaming services, for your entertainment dollars. We cannot go toe to toe with the AMCs and Netflixes of the world, but we are not really trying to. We are trying to offer a different experience. Just as the big-budget, movie-producing machine caters to the multiplexes, they in turn cater back to the studios producing the blockbusters. And as a result, the moviegoing experience becomes more and more homogenized, and the smaller movies get less investment by everyone, including the producers, the studios, the theaters, and then ultimately the audience. So where does that leave movies that are not trying to make a billion dollars? They are increasingly going the streaming route because they might not get seen otherwise.

It's true that lots of folks still prefer going to the movies instead of streaming at home, but how long will that last? Sometimes it is cost-prohibitive. Sometimes it is about comfort. In this current state of lockdown and so many unknowns about what the post-COVID-19 world will look like, it is hard to predict moviegoing tendencies.

We can only bank on the idea that stories are by nature a community experience, and people will always seek out connection. We look for ways to understand each other, and ourselves. We look for ways to relate. And if we can continue to find the stories that provide people with new understanding and new relationships, then they will continue to seek stories. If they continue to seek stories with us, then we will continue to try and provide the best experience possible.

On the Community Building Campus, this experience extends beyond the walls of the theater. Come to our building, and you can have dinner or drinks at the public house. Then stroll through the art gallery or smell the flowers in the florist shop before the movie starts. Grab your popcorn and your glass of wine or beer and take in the big screen. Afterwards, you may want to go next door and try out the brewery while some live music is playing. On a given night, there are any number of things happening that make our community dynamic.

Ultimately, I think this lively space is the result of art being present and a priority. The Community Building Campus provides the community with constant opportunities to invest in art and artists. Whether they are chefs or brewers or florists or sculptors or painters or filmmakers, artists are given an opportunity to share their passions, and people respond to that because we are human, and that's how we connect—through the senses, through sharing the stories that matter to us. Our hope is that audiences will continue to show up because the Magic Lantern—and the entire block—has devoted itself to this human experience and brought it all together in one dynamic place.

CHAPTER SEVENTEEN

Full-Spectrum Leadership

By Nina Simons

Nina is co-founder of Bioneers and serves as its chief relationship strategist and founder of its Everywoman's Leadership program. In collaboration with her teaching partners, Toby Herzlich and Rachel Bagby, she has helped cultivate strong cohorts of women leaders in Spokane.

When I was first acknowledged for my leadership publicly, about nine years after co-founding Bioneers and in my late-thirties, I had conflicting responses. I knew I should be honored, but I didn't like being labeled with that title, didn't believe that I'd earned it, and felt it painted a target on my back. At the same time, I understood how vital it was for all people to aspire to and cultivate themselves towards greater leadership in order to face the massive changes ahead. This inner conflict sent me headlong into an inquiry about how we define leadership. I read scores of texts and transcripts, searching for models I could wholeheartedly aspire to, and then sought to find common themes among the leaders I found most inspiring.

Over time, I realized that our definitions of leadership are inherited and culturally informed. In the U.S., our understanding of what leadership looks like has been largely defined by hierarchical, top-down, and winner-takes-all systems of patriarchy, white supremacy, and capitalism. But I also recognized an emergent leadership, a form we are all co-evolving in this transformational time—one that is far more inclusive, holistic, and integrative of our many human capacities, and one that allows for many differing forms of expression.

My investigation resulted in co-creating an anthology, *Moonrise: The Power of Women Leading from the Heart*, which illustrates the models and core themes that differentiate this new vision for leadership. *Moonrise* synthesizes what I learned: that leaders now are leading from the inside out. In other words, they are in positions of leadership principally because of an internal sense of a calling, purpose, or passion that prompted them, rather than a job title, an inherited power position, a graduate degree, or any other external symbol or conferring of leadership as a role.

By prioritizing relationship before task, these new leaders are reweaving connection among people, places, ideas, and issues. They are renegotiating power, acting from a place of generosity, while lifting up other leaders and sharing authority and power, instead of competing in a zero-sum game.

The new leaders I found in my research weren't all women; some were men. To actively explore and invest in collaborations and partnerships, they tended to lead more from the heart than from the head—integrating head and heart together. They trusted their intuitive and emotional responses and their own passion as a kind of compass that guided their work. In the process, they are restoring the human qualities that have been inaccurately relegated only to the feminine, and to women. This opened up new possibilities, for all of their leadership practices, strategies, and institutions, and cultures.

One term I came to use to summarize this approach is "full-spectrum leadership," a concept that encompasses leaders' diverse and multiple dimensions, skill sets, and perspectives, as well as the potential impacts or consequences to the human or organizational system they're addressing. It recognizes the spectrum of capacities each of us contain as individuals and suggests the ability to access flexibly from a full array of human capacities and approaches. Those capacities and approaches may span from the relational to the analytical, and from more introverted to extroverted. Given the array of cultural identities, orientations, and backgrounds people bring with them, it acknowledges the need for honoring pluralism and appreciating diversity as part of any good organizational evolution.

This concept acknowledges (and some scholars believe) that gendered biases may be among the deepest in the human psyche. We have inherited a mental model of leadership that prioritizes those skills and talents associated with the "masculine" and undervalues those that have been associated with the "feminine." (I tend to use air quotes around "masculine" and "feminine" because of the baggage we carry around those words, and the belief systems and assumptions that we inherited with them.) In a time when the relational skills that women often bring to leadership are required for optimal effectiveness, this conscious rebalancing and reorientation is badly needed for the reinvention of leadership, for both men and women.

Full-spectrum leadership appreciates, values, and integrates the multiple ways of knowing we each encompass: body wisdom, intuition, reasoning, analysis, and emotional or relational intelligences. It involves a flexible and fluid dance between knowing when to lead and when to follow or be receptive; when to generate new ideas or consider new input, and when to take a step back, to pause and reevaluate. It embraces the value of vulnerability, and of transparency and not-knowing, which offers a chance to pause and listen for where other suggestions and solutions may emerge. It embraces the idea of rotating leadership and sharing decision-making authority. It includes an intentional balance of speaking and listening, of offering ideas and deep questioning for feedback loops from another person, or from the community—from the organization or living system you are seeking to affect.

Full-Spectrum Leadership: Harnessing the Masculine & Feminine

As I began to investigate leadership at large—to try to understand and unpack my own negative reaction to being called a leader, and to surface a new definition that I could aspire to—what I found was that the mental model I had inherited was one characterized by what's conventionally seen as "masculine" traits. Although it was one of my innate gifts, within the context of leadership I had very little appreciation of the full value of relationships, of complex and varied interactions both within ourselves, and among ourselves and others—what I now call *relational intelligence*.

I see relational intelligence as the varied ways in which we perceive other peoples' meanings, realities, and perceptions—the cues and clues we notice and use to discern what others actually need or want. Physical posture, tone of voice, level of tension or relaxation, quality of presence—all of these convey meaningful information that is immensely useful when discovering how to relate well to a person, situation, or group and connect with them in a meaningful way. Both men and woman can be relationally intelligent, though I believe that—through a combination of biology and social conditioning—this form of intelligence is often more readily accessible to women.

I began to evaluate things in terms of their balance between masculine and feminine. Discipline, for example, is something I associate with the masculine. In its purest form, discipline can be seen as discipleship. Being rebellious by nature, I spent the first part of my life having an immediate aversion to a rigid affiliation with rules. As I've aged, I've discovered how valuable discipline is as an internal capacity for cultivating my own leadership and for intentionally growing myself into the person I want to become, moment by moment and choice by choice.

Over time, I developed an interior shorthand that I use when navigating the world. My shorthand for the masculine is rigor, being accountable to others and holding myself accountable. My shorthand for the feminine, although it has many different aspects, is compassion. Both within myself and in my work designing a convening or a Bioneers conference, I look toward the balance of head and heart; I hold space for all four human capacities, the physical, emotional, mental, and spiritual; and I cultivate a sense of balancing rigor and compassion in how I seek to offer an integral experience.

We have inherited the unconscious belief that men are masters of "masculine" traits, and women are skillful at the "feminine" ones. This belief no longer serves us. As young people so readily understand now, a gender binary is far too limiting to contain the full expression of our humanity in this time. As all the ancients knew, life is a dance of the yin and yang. We all contain lunar and solar within us, regardless of what gendered body we may be inhabiting. Also, we've inherited some very toxic stereotypes of the masculine and feminine, so it behooves us all to innovate, reinterpret, and claim more liberating identities through which to express ourselves in this time of reinvention.

I draw upon my capacity to have a vector-like focus, which I experience as a masculine trait, one I seek to balance with listening, openness, flexibility, and respect for other perspectives. I've also learned that everything takes longer than you imagine, and my life experience has taught me that "perseverance furthers." Full-spectrum leadership means setting an intention and staying with it while staying open, being willing to regroup and change tactics or strategies but retaining the vision that is central to my motivation.

Decisiveness, another trait that people experience as masculine, has great virtues. Like every other human quality, it is multivalent by nature, which

Nina Simons is co-founder of Bioneers

means it can express consciously or unconsciously. In its "shadow" expression, it can become too rigid. Decisiveness without receptivity can be dictatorial or plutocratic. But there are times when decisiveness is really needed. My ideal is to be able to hear multiple perspectives and adjust my own vision or direction enough to incorporate those perspectives without totally diluting the energy going forward. It's important to expand and adapt, and if necessary, to be willing to change course if someone else's ideas are better. This equilibrium is what I experience as full-spectrum leadership.

Toward Cultivating Full-Spectrum Leaders

The concept of amplifying women's leadership practices came into greater focus for me in 1990, after co-founding Bioneers. Bioneers acts as a fertile hub of social and scientific innovators with practical and visionary solutions for the world's most pressing environmental and social challenges. In 1997, I started programming diverse women leaders around this idea of restoring the feminine to greater balance in ourselves, in our relationships, and in our institutions.

In 2002, through Bioneers, we convened my first gathering of women leaders, called Unreasonable Women for the Earth, inspired by Diane Wilson. That convening, through the work of the participants in the group, eventually led to the co-founding of CodePink: Women for Peace. I didn't have any direct experience to inform me in designing the gathering, but I trusted my intuition, instincts, and my heart to guide me, with support from great allies and facilitators, Diane Haug and Toby Herzlich. I was the connection point for a group of dedicated, changemaker, women leaders who were diverse in every way, who would not otherwise have come together for six days with an intention to weave connections in support of their work. Together, we created the conditions for brainstorming, heartstorming, and potential collaboration among them.

Our societal bias has led to a gross and systemically unequal representation of women in leadership, across all sectors. Since we know that diversity adds resilience to any living system, the lack of women's and people of color's perspectives in our governance and leadership has led us to a deeply corrupt, imbalanced, and brittle system, with little adaptability or accountability to the social and ecological systems it's meant to serve. As President Obama noted, if there were more women in leadership globally, the world would be a far healthier and more peaceful place. United Nations research has revealed that wherever there are more women in leadership, every system improves, from the ecological to the economic, and including health, governance, and education.

A few years after that initial gathering, I got together with Toby Herzlich and Akaya Windwood to co-create a six-day immersive experience for women called Cultivating Women's Leadership (CWL). Toby, Akaya, and I set out to curate a circle of diverse women from various sectors that we imagined could collaboratively strengthen each other to help affect ongoing systemic change. We applied what we had learned about curating circles to encourage transformative learning, which included optimizing diversity among the participants in all its forms—multigenerational, cross-cultural, cross-sectoral, multidisciplinary. By gathering women who could represent such a variety of perspectives, who are often otherwise siloed because of the fracturing nature of our society, we could assemble and cross-pollinate ideas through relationships in a way that we imagined could strengthen each one's efforts for the long haul.

To unpack our approach a little more, part of the structural design of our patriarchally inclined culture means that people often become pigeonholed in their own area of expertise. Artists tend to know artists. Lawyers know other attorneys and judges. Executives know other high-level leadership. The composition of the circle we convened was as important as the vision of what we sought to accomplish.

The program was designed to take women through an experience of intimate exploration, within themselves and in the presence of each other. It simultaneously clarified their individual senses of purpose, assignment, calling, and revealed what women may uniquely bring to leadership. CWL embodied the experience of mutual support, collaboration, and empowerment that a willingness to be vulnerable can bring. It also emphasized the value of connection and mirroring for learning, showing why relationship before task is so essential and powerful.

Over the years, CWL continued to evolve and brought together hundreds of women—including two uniquely place-based cohorts totaling forty women in Spokane.

Cultivating Women's Leadership in Spokane

At first, Jim invested in women's leadership by sending one Spokane woman every year or two to participate in CWL. Then, in 2014, he and another generous donor decided to pool their resources and invite us to help design a CWL experience near Spokane for women from the greater Spokane region.

My colleagues Toby, Rachel Bagby, and I delved into this new challenge. Where we had always brought together women from across the country, this new place-based model would require us to be sensitive to the fact that, after having deep and intimate personal growth experiences together, these women would continue seeing each other on a regular basis. This, of course, was part of the advantage of a place-based model: the relationships forged could act as connective tissue and cultivate a powerful, regional network of women supporting each other in effectively leading change.

The outcomes and impacts of this kind of intensive investment in women's leadership are hard to trace. To understand this, we rely on the testimonies of women themselves. As one woman wrote in a thank-you letter after the intensive:

Thank you for taking a risk and investing in something that has never been done before yet produced life-changing results. Thank you for investing . . . in a place where I believe you're going to see some real return. You have helped to create a new, strong, deep, diverse, beautiful community of Spokane women. Thank you for the opportunity you helped to create for me.

I've never taken a week for myself in such an intentional way. The space that was created by Nina, Toby and Rachel helped me be vulnerable, open, focused, intentional, honest, challenged, and loved. This was quite special. I usually put others first before dealing with my own needs and this retreat forced me to focus on me. The facilitators exceeded my expectations as did the quality of each of the women who I was participating with. I've lived in Spokane for three years and have had a hard time balancing running a nonprofit as the one and only staff person along with building a healthy community outside of work. The new relationships that I've built have and will continue to strengthen me and will help me to create a more full, satisfying, and meaningful life.

Other signs that this leadership intensive has been nourishing a generation of Spokane women leaders is the fact that the women who participated supported a second iteration of the leadership intensive in 2019, which evolved into a form called Women Leading Change. I was not part of this gathering, but Toby, and Rachel—along with a third facilitator, Elsa Menendez—led a six-day leadership intensive for a new cohort. On the final day, most of the original twenty women showed up to connect with the new cohort of twenty, and to explore opportunities for strategic and creative co-conspiring.

The Sheehans are unusual in how they are practicing leadership in Spokane—both by nurturing women leaders and in their own practice of leadership. What I have witnessed over time is that Jim is deeply invested in the Spokane community, and as such, really listens to the feedback and needs of the community. He actually demonstrates this dance of being proactive and receptive in balance. I see him continually invest in the leadership of others. He has consistently worked his way out of a job in the interest of lifting up other leaders. One of the things that has impressed me is that there's nothing perfunctory about how he bestows or delegates leadership. He does it in a whole hearted way that I believe is rare in this world. When he delegates, he gives people room to learn, explore, and make their own mistakes, and he is very gentle and respectful when offering counsel and guidance. He is unusually humble and good at letting go of control.

The Sheehans are also unusual in how they take a long-term view and have fully embraced relationship before task. In other words, they are relating to people in their whole humanity. They are collaborating with people as whole people, not as taskmasters. They are willing to be flexible and adaptive to people's needs as they arise. This respect and reciprocity are central to full-spectrum leadership. Both Jim and Katy embodied it through Cultivating Women's Leadership in Spokane, with an eye toward being cross-sectoral, intergenerational, and multicultural. Jim has embodied it for a long time though his commitment to the law as a nexus and a lever for healthy, progressive, place-based environmental and social change.

Full-Spectrum Leadership and Power

The essence of full-spectrum leadership is that it is deeply respectful of difference and invested in the power of others rather than the power of self. We are living through a time when power relationships are being challenged and upended in a big way in every direction. There is a particular need for models of great leadership in relation to power. What I've been discovering is that, in many ways, confronting who has power, and how that power is used, is a feminist approach to leadership—once we recognize that feminism or a feminist approach isn't about women leading. A feminist approach to leadership is about true equity and complementarity between the masculine and the feminine. It's about including and valuing a pluralism of all people's perspectives and all capacities.

Recalibrating our definition of leadership at this time is integrally bound up with our understanding of power, and so we must shift the conversation to what power is and how it operates. I believe that power is an inherent energetic quality that is abundant in the universe, and that every person has the capacity to exercise power. When we get out of our own way, power courses through us. Too often, we obstruct our own power. As women, many of us are products of a culture that has taught us to undermine our own capacity to exercise power. Our patriarchal bias has us turn to an authoritative father figure for help, when in fact we are all designed to be our own best guides for what wants to come through us.

As soon as the word *philanthropy* comes up, it conjures a conventional modality where the person with the money has the power, and the community does not. What's exciting to me right now are people who are deploying money in ways that are empowering other leaders, movements, and communities. That typically involves a release of decision-making from the philanthropist, and a willingness to not be the sole decider, to share power and relegate authority to the community.

Community development and philanthropy involve the intersection of multiple complex systems. Having the capacity to take in, assess, and consider the next best move for the health of the community or communities, in relation to monetary flows, is an emergence of full-spectrum leadership—one that considers power differentials, social structures, race, class, ethnicity, and identity. It is possible for leaders to deploy money in ways that empower communities, but again, for this to happen, philanthropists must release decision-making and power.

It is rare for a white man with resources to not conflate his power with use of resources. Jim is deeply caring and truly invested in what's good for the whole, and his relationship to money and power reflects this, which is unusual and a big deal. He is an important model for others in that way. He is also an example of how to defy founder's syndrome. He has very conscientiously used resources—and the influential authority and privileges that they confer—in ways that are quite fluid. He has avoided the trap of wanting to reify, control, or contain; instead, he has identified people he trusts to share responsibility and leadership in generous and trusting ways.

There are new movements and philanthropic models emerging around the decolonization of wealth, a concept which requires us to relinquish presumptive beliefs that often accompany our white, dominant culture: that the person with money knows what's best. In fact, nobody who is outside the community can really know what's best. I think we are in a time of an immense paradigm shift in terms of the people on the ground really being the only ones who can know what's needed. Jim has modeled some of those practices, sharing power with the community, and really listening.

Another version of philanthropic power-shift we see rising elsewhere is regranting funds. For example, Marion Weber has been innovating and practicing "Flow Funding" for many years, an innovative form of philanthropy which encourages money to flow spontaneously through the hands of new funders. In Flow Funding, donors entrust their money to social innovators and visionaries to give away. It infuses trust, discovery, and adventure into the funding process, and increases the number of philanthropists in the world by empowering social innovators, healers, and visionaries to give away money. The concept of Flow Funding stemmed from a quest to democratize philanthropy and explore alternative ways to donate money. This is one of the purest models for philanthropy that I've ever seen, and it's also recreating the gift economy that nature and many Indigenous cultures have long practiced.

We know that our economic system has failed the vast majority of people. As we look to transform it, one of my favorite models comes from the gift economy, and many Native Peoples' models of resource-sharing. In many of their cultures, the one who is most respected is the one who gives away most of their belongings. In ours, it's been the one who amasses the most for themselves. The gift economy relies upon the relationships among people to share what's needed, assuming that—as with nature—there is abundance if only we share it appropriately. Shifting from a me-based economic model to one that encompasses the good of the commons, the community, or the whole system, is one of the next greatest challenges we have to confront. Fortunately, with a generation of remarkable, full-spectrum leaders on the rise, this shift is already under way.

CHAPTER EIGHTEEN

Organizational Leadership from the Heart

By Mary Alberts

Mary lived and worked in China for years as a human resources director for a Chinese-German multinational company before moving to Spokane, where she attended Gonzaga University's Doctoral Program in Leadership and later served as director of Whitworth University's Graduate School of Business. She has been Jim's partner for almost fifteen years, and her depth of professional expertise made her a natural consultant and adviser in the evolution of the Community Building Campus.

Jim and I now look like we're cut of the same cloth—black active wear, shocking white hair, and a matched limp as we walk the local golf courses, dreaming up new projects for our favorite nonprofits. But when we met for the first time, over fifteen years ago, we appeared to have very little in common. I was, undoubtedly, wearing a nicely tailored suit and high heels, while Jim would have been dressed like an aging hippie.

From every appearance, we came from different worlds. But both of us had grown up in second-generation immigrant, working-class families and were intimately familiar with the challenges faced by first-in-college offspring. However, I worked my way through college, Jim benefited from the support of a generous aunt who recognized the value of a good education. Aunt Verle clearly had no idea just how significant a role she would ultimately play. Jim used his education and law degree to support the struggles of those who lacked voice in an imperfect criminal justice system. I, on the other hand, used my education to prove that I could rise above the limitations of my birth. I spent hours trying to convince my pro-union mother, a graduate of diners and factory lines, that globalism was key to our future. Although she is no longer here to say, "I told you so," I now believe she may have been on to something.

Jim and I met around 2006 at an innovative talk on green business hosted by the Community Building. At that time, the idea of green business seemed new—at least it was not something that very many people practiced in our area. As director of the graduate programs at Whitworth University's School of Global Commerce and Management, I regularly taught courses that would benefit from a deeper exploration of the interplay between business and the health of our environment. When I read in the newspaper that Kevin Danaher, founder of Global Exchange of San Francisco, would be speaking in Spokane, I was very interested. Global Exchange envisioned people-centered globalization—the concept of valuing the rights of workers and the sustainability of our planet. No one in Spokane's higher education circles talked about this, and I instinctively knew it was deeply important.

For over thirty years, I had primarily worked with conservative businessmen (and they were almost always men) and old-school economists. Concerned primarily with the health and well-being of investors, these were not worker- or planet-friendly bosses and colleagues. Their business values were focused on a single bottom line, corporate and shareholder profit. This strategy was seldom good for the workers (who we claim are the "heart of the company"), the clients (whom we serve), or for the planet itself. Jim was the driving force behind a diverse community of folks in a part of town I had never even visited, and they were all working toward a common goal to make things more environmentally and communally friendly, which was a really interesting vision to me. Here were concepts I had only read about being put into practice in my own community.

Most surprising was walking into the Community Building for the first time. Instead of the usual monochrome sterility of most business environments, I was wrapped in the warmth of glowing woods, battling textures, and color, color, color. There was art on the walls—not the kind that blend in with the décor, but the kind that make you want to walk up, breath-close, and examine every detail. More importantly, never before in my business and education career had I entered a space and felt so instantly surrounded by professionals who shared my values. I felt both like a fish out of water and a person who had come home at last. A man with warm, smiling eyes and an awkward smile approached me with a glass of wine and a welcome. Introducing himself as one of the team members who developed this lovely space and brought the speaker to Spokane, he offered me the glass of wine and extended an invitation to enjoy my evening. After the talk, he returned to my seat, and suggested I "show up" for a post-discussion event at a friend's home on the South Hill, which I decided to attend. It was one very stimulating evening!

Jim and I didn't have our first date until much later. Taking a walk through Riverside Park, we talked nonstop about our libraries and the writers who had shaped our thinking over the years. Just about every book or literary emphasis in his library matched my own. As we walked along the shores of the river, watching the rapids fight their way through the Bowl and Pitcher rock formations, Jim discussed the challenges his anchor organization, the Center for Justice, faced daily, working to stop the pollutants that poisoned the fish and wildlife of the Spokane River. He shared frightening stories of deadly PCBs, paper mill pollution, and silver mining legacies. He shared his sadness for the number of children, elderly, and asthmatics who struggled each year with the smoke coming from the annual field burns. He obviously loved the Spokane River and the surrounding golden Palouse wheat fields and felt it his obligation to protect those who wanted to safely swim and fish in the river, while breathing fresh clean air. Here was someone compatible with my own philosophies, and I wanted to get to know him better. Although Jim believed "business" and the drive for profit were the main culprits in these environmental travesties, I continually argued that the business community could also be a strong partner in solving such problems. It was the first of many passion-fueled disagreements to come over the way the world works.

For decades, I had been part of the chamber of commerce crowd and a member of a number of business-oriented organizations. There was always a lot of talk about being more profitable and making Spokane stronger from an economic standpoint. But it was rare to be involved in conversations about how Spokane could be a more livable city, a more caring community, and a better friend to its workforce. People seldom talked about the human side of commerce in business circles, or in the classroom, unless it was to decry the cost. I had been feeling the void that such profit-centered discussions create for a very long time. To suddenly find someone not only talking about social and environmental justice in business, but also actually doing something about it, was exciting to me. I started attending more events with Jim, gratified by his

Jim Sheehan and Mary Alberts

community-centered approach, and what a refreshing change it was from the circles in which I had been moving. Through my growing love for Jim, and this unique and inclusive community, I began to feel a connection with Spokane and started thinking of it as my home instead of just another temporary move in life and career.

Over time, I learned more about the Center for Justice, which stood up for those who often lacked the financial and political power to defend and protect themselves. I appreciated how Jim was addressing environmental issues by supporting other sustainability-minded organizations and showcasing some of the greenest commercial buildings in Washington State. I loved his vision for the Community Building, of creating a place of beauty and affordability for a number of nonprofits previously scattered throughout the city. His focus on synergy, encouraging these organizations to find common ground and to avoid duplication through shared resources and talent, made so much sense to me. Jim further believed that employees and clients of nonprofits deserved to be treated with dignity, enjoying a space that honored them with both beauty and convenience. He was committed to the idea that how we are treated strongly impacts how we treat each other—how we react to our world and, subsequently, what we contribute back to it.

When we first got together, I didn't see Jim, and those closest to him, as particularly effective collaborators on a broader scale. I was a firm believer that you can accomplish much more if you find the right partners with whom to collaborate—especially those who may see things a little differently. There was some resistance to collaborating with groups or individuals that Jim and his team viewed as "the establishment." The Community Building had wonderful internal collaborations but not many with outside organizations, including business associations, developers, and city government. Over time, I watched Jim open up to other perspectives and begin to welcome the input and support of others outside his community. He didn't always agree, but he learned to understand what interests others have at stake that might make them resistant to his ideas and values, or to make decisions he considered clearly wrong. This evolving willingness to explore how to work with those who think radically differently from him, in order to make change happen, has given him and his team a stronger voice in downtown development.

Overall, Jim has a much deeper and broader perspective today. I'd like to think this was partly my influence, but it may just be a result of growing older and a little wiser. He has gone from an anti-establishment, "stick-it-to-the-man" mentality to a "we're-stronger-together" mindset. That's been an important and positive shift in our relationship because, in so many ways, I was "the man," given my career history and centrist politics. In some ways, I represented the very things against which he had rebelled for decades. It gave us the opportunity to be both student and teacher to each other.

The Community Building is a big, democratic experiment in terms of people management. It gets messy and it's definitely not efficient. Admittedly, Jim's leadership style has always been a bit of a mystery to me. Influenced by my years in human resource management, I'm a strong believer that people want to be trusted and inspired, but they also long for boundaries and quality guidance. Done right, it can make one's job so much easier. Jim, on the other hand, has always described himself as a hands-off idea guy. He prefers to give people the opportunity to make a role for themselves, encouraging them to engage their own passions and strengths, defining their own role in the organization. He'll nudge people to follow their hearts in whatever direction works for them in terms of contribution to the community. Coming from a business background, I've struggled with this loose approach, as it sometimes feels disorganized, unpredictable, and disconnected to the mission. Freedom and self-definition are great, but they can have unexpected consequences in the workplace when people struggle to find their direction. Some folks, like Kizuri's original owner, Kim Harmson, flourished under loose guidelines. Other projects, however, have been less successful, usually because the primary individual failed to truly grasp the Community Building concept and Jim's foundational philosophy of One.

Resident business owners commit to fair trade practices and locally grown and produced products. Wages are set to provide a decent living, and the need for recreation and family flexibility is honored. Sometimes it falls short of its ideals, ending in failure for some and disappointment for others. Other times, magical things happen. Like any organization, staff and tenants may bicker over whose responsibility it is—because things are so loosely defined—while at the same time teaming up to find creative (and humane) solutions to space allocations, building upkeep, and organization development. Jim regularly funded inclusive happy hours and personal and professional development retreats to grow the cohesiveness of the community. The Community Building tenants work together to address neighborhood challenges such as homelessness, security, landscaping, and traffic flow, making the neighborhood more beautiful and safe for all. When people like and respect each other, they accomplish incredible things together.

Jim is the right kind of leader for such a messy experiment. He's trusting and does not need to be in control. He brings enthusiasm to leadership. If there is something he embraces, he brings others in and gets them excited, too. His leadership is fundamentally inspirational. For example, when he started the Center for Justice, he made himself available to young lawyers to discuss what it means to practice law with compassion, and what that looks like in the real world. He spoke passionately about the need to look past the crime and see the individual—lessons he learned as a public defender. This was challenging in the days prior to the Smart Justice movement. The prevalent attitude throughout Spokane's criminal justice and court systems was to punish, not rehabilitate, and Jim saw this very differently. This attitude continues to live through his Community Building team as they humanely manage the challenges of a growing downtown homeless population due to addiction and the escalation of untreated mental health issues.

Over the years, I have grown to appreciate Jim's style more and more, and to realize that effective leadership manifests in a variety of forms and over differing timeframes. And in fairness, I've changed, too. I've grown to value what Jim's been trying to do all these years, and respect how differently he tries to operate. I've asked him often if difference, just for the sake of being different, is always a good thing. What are you really trying to accomplish? I'd observed that sometimes "doing it differently" could frustrate Jim's team because they didn't know the rules, and they weren't sure how to help organically create the rules with him. But again, that may just be my HR background talking. Jim leaned on his community to keep creating and trusting. He regularly reminded me that social transformation takes time and that the results—the deep, lasting results—are not always immediately apparent. Jim was investing in a better future for Spokane, and it required patience.

Most of the time, Jim feels good about his influence and what he's accomplished. On occasion, however, it weighs on him when he sees the inevitable downside of any social experiment: infighting, triangulation, pettiness, and all those things that come when you invite a diverse group of people into your vision. When he first received his inheritance, I think he had a dream that, by doing things differently, everyone who embraced this vision would be different as well. That's been true in most cases, but not all. People occasionally develop a "Jim complex" and become too concerned about pleasing him, when all he really wants is for them to take what he has given and invest it back into the community. A few have taken advantage of Jim's trust and generosity, which has been frustrating and a little heartbreaking. Fortunately, those cases have been rare, and the negative impact on the community was usually short-lived. Even when projects or businesses have failed, Jim has never given up on the individuals who made the effort. He always seems to understand that to fail is to learn, and he wants these friends to go back out into the world prepared to try again and help someone else.

Jim has always known that people would not carry on the vision exactly as he saw it, but he's hoped that, in spirit and in heart, a core group would carry the vision forward—that the idea of Community Building would grow and grow, and that the whole community would become more connected and stronger as a result. And so, when people behave in ways that people do, regardless of the social experiment, this discourages him a bit. Unbridled optimism may be a pitfall for idealists in any situation and leaves them vulnerable to disappointment. Over time, Jim has gotten better at breaking away from an overwhelming sense of expectation and obligation, and has begun to let go. A maturing core staff, and the involvement of his son, Joe, and daughter, Katy, have helped him make this transition.

When I see him with his kids—again, a "management" style you might think would never work—they clearly love, trust, and admire their dad. I can assure you that they had a rather loose upbringing that would strike terror in the hearts of most "helicopter" parents today. But look how they've turned out! They're great kids. They are fantastic human beings. They've married wonderful partners, and the grandkids are equally delightful, appreciated for their kindness and thoughtfulness towards others. They are people who are good additions to our world, which is what matters most. That's why, when his dear friend and long-time foundation director, Patty Gates, announced her resignation, I suggested to Jim that he consider his daughter, Katy, for the position. Jim was totally surprised, as it is usually best to avoid nepotism in an organization. But he listened and responded, "Well, tell me why."

I'm usually the first person who would suggest keeping family out of things, but I reminded Jim that he was aging and starting to pull away from the day-to-day operations. I had gotten to know his kids and thought Katy would handle the whole Community Building project responsibly. Who better to run his foundation than someone who has a deep investment in it? Otherwise, when he goes, he'll have two kids who own buildings but have little understanding of the special environment he helped to create there. If they were not engaged in some meaningful way, Katy and Joe would inherit something they may not perceive as much of a gift—a weird kind of real estate that comes with a social headache and not much of a moneymaker. Here was a great opportunity to see if one of his children could become invested, not only in the running of the buildings, but also in the nurturing of a dynamic community. Several years down the road, both Katy and Joe are integral parts of the Community Building, taking Jim's vision to new levels of community commitment and engagement.

The tendency to isolate as a "unique" community has diminished as Jim's daughter and son have become more involved in the administration of the Community Building. They exhibit a willingness to reach out throughout the Spokane community and form new partnerships. The ongoing challenge, however, is how to partner without being co-opted. The introduction of more commercial enterprises into the buildings indicates that Jim no longer sees for-profit business as the enemy. I think his attitude has softened to something like, "We all shop, we all have needs, we all do these things, so let's open up and embrace this commonality, but in a healthier, more people-centered, and environmentally friendly way." Of course, he did some of this from the start with the opening of Kizuri, Blueprints for Learning, and the Main Market. He put his own money behind these ideas and the people he believed in, with a variety of results—some good, others less successful. With a space like the Saranac Commons, he is starting to invest in businesses that are more sustainable on their own, which is important to the health of any community. But trust me, they are on board with the Community Building way. Jim now accepts that profit is an important part of the equation, as long as it is not the only—or even the primary—consideration.

There is much pleasure in the legacies of human growth. When Jim sees someone whose tuition he has covered graduate from university, or an employee who has achieved a personal goal they would not have otherwise, or a successful entrepreneur to whom he lent seed money, that really builds him up. It gives him deep pleasure and gratitude for the good fortune that made all of this possible. He feels like he's investing in the whole world when he invests in one person at a time. When I think about Jim's legacy, I think about sand mandalas, those beautiful pieces of art that are temporary and taken by the wind. That's the image that comes to mind because that's what it is for him. He sees everything as impermanent. That's part of his philosophy of life. We are One, and change is the only given. I think that's why, when relationships in the whole, messy Community Building experiment get really hard, he can just let it go, knowing that the inherent goodness will continue to exist. It's at the core of what he truly believes and, thanks to him, what I have also come to believe.

The most important thing to know about Jim is that he is very driven by love. Deep love. He practices it on many different levels. On the meta level, he loves this world. He has not, nor will he ever, give up on it. He continues to actively support environmental and social causes and, as you might imagine, has a few strong opinions on each. On a local level, I've watched his ongoing investment in the people who have come into his life through the Community Building. He's helped them start new businesses, educate their children, buy a home, or just make it through a rough patch in life. There have been times when I've thought, "Well, you should just take this person off your guest list." But he doesn't do it. He's a very loyal guy. If he believes in you, he stays with you. He is with you through the tough times, and this has been a life raft for struggling friends and neighbors. And what is most rewarding is that many have gone on to help others in similar ways.

I don't think Jim puts a lot of time into thinking about how he's going to be remembered in a month, a decade, or a generation. The only thing he really hopes for is that whatever spirit or wisdom—whatever joy was gained in this process by the folks involved—that these good things will continue to be passed on to the people in their lives, through their employees, through their partners, through their children. I think that's the legacy he looks for, more than worrying about whether the Community Building will be the Community Building (as he envisioned it) in a decade. Over time, those who have been a part of the founding and growth of the Community Building have moved into other organizations, other states, and even other countries. They take the seeds of Community Building with them into their new communities. In so many ways, the legacy already is.

CHAPTER NINETEEN

The Community Building Legacy

By Katy Sheehan

Katy is a graduate of the City University of New York School of Law and a former staff attorney with the Fair Housing Center of Washington. She is the daughter of Jim Sheehan and the executive director of the Community Building Foundation, which is dedicated to empowering local organizations that help the Spokane community experience justice, vibrancy, and sustainability.

I first learned to think of legacy on a timeline. In Western culture, after someone does something special or creates something beautiful, we look at their life work and measure their effect on the world. We calculate the money they donated or create a scholarship in their name. Their stories, written in past tense, become a retrospective way to honor lives well-lived. However, in a supportive community, legacy doesn't have a beginning or end, and it doesn't involve just one person. Instead, legacy is the continuous cycle of people investing in their community and their work—organizing protests and writing policy around values, cleaning floors, and fixing window latches. No matter the job, all the work is important and necessary.

As a successor to my dad in the Community Building enterprise, it has fallen to me to try to explain our legacy. Describing the story of the Community Building—how it began, how it has evolved, and how we envision its future—

turns out to be a difficult task. My dad invested in something beautiful at the Community Building, but it took countless people also investing in the vision of this place to build community in Spokane. I, too, am one of the investors because I participate in this complex, loving, and imperfect place. This is where I have come of age professionally, built deep friendships, and where I am choosing to introduce my children to the world.

This book is packed full of stories about people who work here and invest in the community in ways that go above and beyond their job descriptions, and there are multitudes of other stories to share about the other ways people have been generous with their skills and knowledge. We are all investing in this place by leading, participating with, and supporting each other. We may all have our different areas of focus, but we see every day how our work interconnects and overlaps. This is why it's hard to talk about a legacy that has a beginning and end or that gets attributed to one person's ideas when so many people have, over the years, poured themselves into their work here. We are all continuously making this place special and beautiful. We are all constantly building a legacy here.

In addition to the social notion of legacy, we must still have a clear plan for the physical spaces where legacy plays out every day: the buildings. There is the very real fact that at the end of my dad's life, there are assets that will be passed down to my brother and me, as well as to our family's foundation. This requires preparation, management, and practical estate planning.

When it comes to legacy, there are three main questions I get asked regularly:

1. What is the estate plan?
2. How do you scale a project like this?
3. How do you make it financially stable?

I'll tackle each question with the blend of cyclical and linear thinking that we've needed to balance our values with the practical realities of working in a capitalistic system, which does not prioritize the flexibility, compassion, and creativity it takes to build community.

What Is the Estate Plan?

Estate planning is hard for me, as it probably is for everyone, because it means contemplating the death of my father. Estate planning requires really tough conversations that, at the end of the day, are so speculative they sometimes feel like they're not worth the effort. How could we ever control the future anyway? How many times has an estate with an "airtight will" been fought over in the courts? Is what my dad wanted at the time he created his will truly the best thing to do in some future situation? These are impossible questions that tend to lead me to frustration and seemingly justified procrastination.

After all the years we've spent discussing the future in the context of estate planning, I only know two things for sure. First, my brother and I understand my dad's values and we share them; second, I cannot completely control the future, so staying flexible is key. For example, my dad does not want the majority of his wealth to go to his children because he doesn't believe in the patrimonial capitalist system that keeps wealth tightly locked away within family systems. My brother and I agree that we do not need that kind of wealth to thrive. Instead, the Community Building Foundation will receive most of my dad's financial assets so that it can continue supporting the flexible, grassroots philanthropy that we believe in. However, we've learned over the years that it is complicated and legally restrictive when a foundation owns property because it has to be used in accordance with the IRS's definition of charitable benefit, which is narrow. For example, John Bjorkman (Chapter 14) mentions how it's challenging to lease to a revenue-generating operation, like the Saranac Pub, under the foundation model. And yet, we have seen that promoting diversity creates vibrant and hyper-local opportunities for businesses, nonprofits, and our co-op to support one another. From catering events, to applying for grants together, to contracting for services, this ecosystem allows organizations to easily build and maintain beneficial partnerships.

As John also describes, it was important to maintain flexibility so that my dad could dispatch his money in creative, unconventional ways. Since this is a part of his legacy that my brother and I wish to continue, and for the buildings to continue to be a flexible asset that can be adapted for a future purpose or use, then it makes sense for them to be owned by an individual or a company. My brother and I have decided to commit to this community's mission, which means that we are building a collaborative estate plan that we are all open to changing and shifting. And in order to do that, we will own the company that owns the building.

I've read enough estate planning cases to know that trusting in a discussion like that seems foolhardy and naïve, and part of me thinks that we are. We will never be accountable in a courtroom in this kind of model where we all agree to keep the mission intact and use a flexible model. But there are other ways to be accountable than going to court. If we abandon the community and use these spaces only to build our own wealth, that hypocrisy will be called out, and our community would likely reject us in a major way. We might walk away with wealth—and I know some people think that's not a bad deal and affords more choices than most people get to make—but that is a lonely and shameful thought to me.

We are not only inheriting a substantial asset; we are also inheriting a complex network of relationships that form a vibrant community. This community already has immeasurable value to me because I have been investing in it for twenty years. In some ways, because my brother and I have also been investing in this community for so long, it will be a formality when the assets are transferred. We are choosing to continue what we are already doing, to keep supporting the cycles of people doing their important work.

To make up for the fact that we do not have a board of directors, our staff acts as the conduit for understanding and representing our community in our decision-making. Part of everyone's job is to maintain healthy working relationships with tenants and partners so that all our staff can help determine how best to maintain the buildings for our community. For now, we have found a balance between the need for flexibility and stewarding with the community. There is still tension between participating with the community while also having all the decision-making power that comes with owning the spaces. I can't completely resolve this conflict because of the structures of our current economic system. The conflict between community input and needing to operate practically and efficiently motivates me to work on changing those structures so that more equity is possible, and we have tried to organize our resources so that they support these efforts for the long haul. That is the work the people in our community invest in every day as they build their businesses or organize policy initiatives—supporting the leadership in communities of color, building wealth among the poor, toppling the structures that hold people back from their full potential.

That our estate plan entails a version of nepotism is a source of both shame and pride for me. On the one hand, I worry that I don't deserve to be in a position of leadership, and on the other, I'm proud that my family has chosen to support nonprofits and small businesses. This tension keeps me humble and motivates me to do the best work I can for my community. It provides me with the drive to stay in a supportive role and reminds me that my voice does not always need to be pushed up to the mic. It helps me step into boardrooms that others can't get into and then try to bring people in with me who would normally be left out. I'm here to help manage the everyday crises that come up when doors stop working or the roof leaks. I help navigate tough relationship issues among community partners and use my legal education to help folks think through sticky issues. I try to do these things in the background so that community leaders can take on issues like racial justice or climate change directly, while I worry about that leaky roof.

How Do You Scale a Project Like This?

My colleague and friend, Sandy Williams, is a quiet, unassuming, and wickedly strategic thinker, as well as a great listener. All these qualities make her a great journalist. I was excited to get to know her because I'd been hearing about her for a few years as the editor of *The Black Lens*, our local Black community's monthly paper. For about a year, four of us met at a local coffee shop with really hard chairs next to the Spokane County Courthouse to work on a writing project. It involved a case where a white man, who confessed to a vigilante-type murder of a Black man, was nevertheless acquitted by an all-white Spokane jury. We were all hoping to spark a community conversation about racism through the project.

After a year of working together, half of the group didn't show up to a meeting, and it was becoming clear we were losing steam. Sandy and I were the only ones there that day, so we drank our coffee together, chatting for the first time just the two of us. During our conversation, she mentioned the idea of *The Black Lens* buying a building in the East Central neighborhood. My ears perked right up when she said, "I don't really have a plan, and I don't know how I'll do it, but I have this vision, and it just feels right." Before the end of the conversation, we had arranged for me and the general contractor we work with at the CBC to look at a space to see if the building had "good bones." A couple weeks later, we toured the building that would become the Carl Maxey Center (CMC).

Fast forward three years. Our writing project has been forever shelved, but the CMC is in phase two of its development. The Carl Maxey Center is a technology innovation hub. It is sustainable, and it works to expand cultural, educational, and economic opportunities for Spokane's African American community. All these values align with our mission at the Community Building, and we are proud to be a supportive partner. Further, the community conversation on systemic racism is under way, and the CMC is a leading voice.

Katy Sheehan, executive director of the Community Building Foundation, with her sons

While the CBC's part in supporting the Carl Maxey Center's development was small compared to the vast amount of work Sandy, the board of *The Black Lens*, and the East Central community provided to pull resources together, we did a lot in the beginning, before there was a groundswell of momentum. The Community Building Foundation offered significant funding, our experience, and our relationships. Sandy was able to leverage a huge amount of public funds through the early private donations, of which we were a part. We also connected her with architect Patsy O'Connor (Chapter 3) who had loads of experience designing community spaces with sustainability in mind. She eventually became the designer of the Carl Maxey Center as well. I attended some of the early grant writing information sessions, provided letters of support for grants, and continue to serve on their advisory board.

When we stopped meeting for coffee, I spent a short minute lamenting the lost time in that coffee shop, developing an abandoned writing project. Then it dawned on me that the relationship building and the conversations we had over the course of that year was the getting-to-know-you part of the work. Without that year, I don't think we would have trusted each other to work together on something WAY bigger than a piece of writing.

This is how I see the Community Building "scaling." Spokane, frankly, doesn't need another CBC, and I don't think we could do it again anyway. But I see community building spaces happening in lots of ways around Spokane. We now have the Carl Maxey Center (Black community), Spark Central (arts community), Terrain (arts), If You Could Save Just One (at-risk-youth community), SPECTRUM (LGBTQ+ community), Spokane FAVS (religious community), Fellow Coworking and other shared-space community-focused projects. And then there are the places that are older than our space, like the Native Project, and the community centers in Northeast, East Central, West Central, South Hill, Corbin, etc. Our idea to build community is not new; it is learned from Indigenous, religious, and civil rights movement thinkers and mystics, just to name a few. We try to remember that in our twenty years of being, we cultivated a balance of new learning and a wellspring of deep knowledge. We try to stay flexible in our newness while we remain grounded in our roots of experience.

These groups are developing because people need community. But they don't need us to do it for them. Spokane does not need a franchised CBC template. In fact, I don't think any community needs our franchise. But what they could use is support in the form of resources, experience, and relationships because these things help communities create something they need and want for themselves. Our legacy is to continue to grow relationships with and among our community partners, where we share information and learn from one another to help provide supportive and mutual benefit.

How Do You Make it Financially Stable?

A lot of folks have asked me this. They ask me as if we don't already know the answer: cut costs and raise rent. I think people want to believe that you can do all the good things we do and still break even because capitalism says you can have it all. Or, that you can do well by doing good, I don't think you can, entirely. In the real estate market as it stands, you can't rent offices at market rate, let alone below market, and still provide living wages and medical benefits to cleaning, security, and administrative staff and their families, along with the other benefits we provide for free to tenants. These include free common and meeting spaces, a professional development series, monthly lunches, access to quality child care, holiday parties, community breakfasts, and occasional retreats and off-site trainings. Connecting people the way we do costs money, and in this system you don't break even at market-rate rent because the market doesn't support these "intangibles."

For nonprofits, these intangibles are the things that funders, both private and public, often don't perceive as clear deliverables. Professional development and providing food at events are the first things to go when belts tighten, and yet those are the first things we should do to take care of people who work hard. I have no idea how many relationships we've built thanks to Mac 'n' Cheese Mondays, our monthly tenant lunch series, but I know it's a lot because of my own experiences of getting to know folks at those lunches. For example, when Terri Anderson of the Tenants Union of Washington State did a presentation about her work during one of our lunch programs, she said the Tenants Union was looking for board members. I got in touch with her afterwards, and we've been working together ever since, even after I cycled off their board.

We do not collect rents that equal our expenses. We've chosen, instead, to supplement our rental income with what we make in capital investments (the stock market). So, technically, we break even because we use our income from the stock market to offset the costs of running the CBC the way that we do. This system is technically sustainable as long as the stock market doesn't completely tank. Our philosophy is that if the stock market takes a permanent dive, there are probably larger societal issues than our rent structures. The result is that our family is not building our wealth the way that we could.

Financial sustainability is a funny thing for me because it generally implies responsibility. It means that we are being smart, and smart usually means building wealth, the implication being that you can do even more good with it. I'm not sure that's a complete picture because if we were to run these spaces in a "financially responsible" way, we would have to cut costs and raise rents. It would follow that smaller nonprofits would be forced to move to another space, and small businesses would have a harder time getting off the ground.

Ultimately, it's about asking yourself important questions. Assuming that you don't need to grow in net worth forever, what is enough? Whatever "enough" means, that is where you start adding benefits for others on your own dime. If we don't subsidize the campus with our own wealth, it means that my family, which has plenty, would continue to grow in net worth while other families with less would struggle more, and that does not seem like sustainability to me. We are constantly fluctuating between living our values and dealing with practical realities. While we don't worry about growing our personal wealth, we still try to responsibly steward the resources we manage, which means we still participate in a capitalistic system.

We believe that legacy in the work of community building is happening right now. We try to be present to whomever or whatever is before us, but we also prepare for the future. To balance these tensions, we turn to our relationships to guide us toward life inside a legacy of love, but not perfection. Our experience is that people who feel secure in their community, who are co-investors, will cycle together through the inevitable tensions that come with the good and bad times. The legacy of being together means that my children will never be alone in the world, even once I'm gone. That my children, with the children of this community, may grow up and live on in a legacy of love is more valuable to me than any bank account I could pass on when I die. I know my dad feels this way too because I'm surrounded by the relationships he's cultivated with so many people who hold and care for me now.

Acknowledgments

Thank you, Jim, for the opportunity to collaborate on this book, and for asking what I believe to be some of the most important questions of our time: How much is enough? What's possible?

Matt and Teako, your unconditional positivity, playfulness, and love have seen me through everything, including this. Thank you, Mom and Dad, for letting me fancy myself many things over the years. Some of them have stuck.

To Rebecca Mack, for editing support that enlivened my academic proclivities, and for always asking questions that helped bring more into the light. To Anna, for editing support and for thinking of me when scouting for a replacement. To Heidi, for helping me tighten and think through the proposal, and to Olivia, for assisting with many transcriptions. To Paul Lindholdt, for his careful editing of the advance review copy and his generous endorsement.

To Mary, Joe, and Katy for being forthright about the complexities of the family business. To the rest of the Community Building team, past and present—Pat, Warrin, Aung, Shelley, Austen, Doug, and others—for constant personal and professional support.

To Toby, for being a thought companion and mentor through the years. To Sayre, for helping me learn how to tell this story to a wider audience. To Nina, Kenny, and the whole Bioneers crew for introducing me to the origins of much of Jim's inspiration.

To Jon and Latah Books for saying yes, believing in the power of anthologies, and bringing together a chorus of voices. To the acquisition editors from other publishing houses who pushed me to refine the scope of this book.

To Katie Edwards, Leena Waite, Saul Ettlin, and others from the Nonprofit Center Network, for showing us we had colleagues in this space and for giving us more ways to talk about our work.

To my MFA instructors and classmates, for showing me that I wasn't a writer yet, but that I could be. To my GWU profs—Hobbs, Theado, Land, Hemmy, Davis, Jones, and others—for teaching me how to think, and giving me my start. To Ms. Bell for encouraging me to take time for my craft. To Dr. Gayle Bolt Price, for believing in raw ability that would take decades to evolve into talent. I miss you and still want to make you proud.

To my Wenatchee crew for celebrating the incremental milestones of a big project with me. To Natalia, for all the check-ins with wine and garden dinners. To Jill, Molly, and Rafa for giving me a place to live when I needed a home.

Kia ora (Maori greeting) to my C-Lab friends for giving me community as I took time away from my regular life to think and write. To the social innovators and creatives in Christchurch who inspired me (especially the good people at Akina, FESTA, and Ministry of Awesome), and the Southern Alps traverse team for drawing me away from the computer and into the hills.

To Luke, Jaquelyn, and the Treatment team for being great collaborators on our website. Those conversations helped me frame and conceptualize the book.

To Annie and Mark at Measure Meant for giving the insights I acquired while editing this book a professional home.

To the contributors for being so generous with their time, insights, and personal stories. Talking about the hard is part of painting the full scope of the good, and you all took this challenge on gracefully. To everyone who read the advance review copies and provided edits and endorsements."

To Bob Zeller for showing up and documenting countless events. Your Green Progressive Archive was an inspiration.

Finally, I would like to thank every person I formally interviewed whose brilliance did not have the chance to unfold on these pages, including: Dan Baumgarten, Laurence Brahm, Timothy Connor, Ben Cribb, Kevin Danaher, Chris DeForest, Dan Dvorak, Rick Eichstaedt, Lupito Flores, Lars Gilbert, Charlie Gurche, Bart Haggin, John Hancock, Jeremy Hansen, Kate Hansen, Hollis Higgins, Jill Johnson, Karen Lindholdt, Thomas Linzey, David Loy, Anne Martin, Dave Martin, Liz Moore, Nancy Nelson, Rusty Nelson, Lolly O'Neil, Teresa Pisani, Lori Rockroth, Nancy Schaub, Kathy Thamm, Stuart Valentine, Steve Wells, Sandy Williams, and Megan Wingo. Your insights provided valuable context that made my inquiry deeper and more nuanced. I'm also indebted to the hundreds of casual interactions and thoughtful conversations that formed my experience of working on the CBC. It is, of course, the accumulation of these moments that builds community.

Index

207

Community Building Children's Center (CBCC) 26, 51, 77-87, 117
Community Building Foundation (CBF) 72, 120-130, 146, 150, 153, 157, 194, 196, 199
the co-op. *See Main Market Co-op*
countercultural 4, 10, 16
Cultivating Women's Leadership (CWL) 178, 179, 181

D
defensible space 33–35
Downtown Spokane Partnership 56

E
Eastern Washington University 1, 126
Envision Spokane 131–143
estate planning 195, 196
Expo '74 21, 50

F
fair trade 23, 34, 63, 78, 109–118, 189
Flores, Lupito 90, 93, 94, 96

G
Ganesh Himal Trading Company 109, 110, 115
Gates, Patty 4, 120–130, 191
geothermal 46, 47
Global Folk Art 112, 115, 116
Gonzaga University 51, 66, 128, 184
grassroots 4, 19, 135, 139, 159, 196
Greater Spokane Progress (GSP) 72, 125, 126, 128, 159
green energy 42, 44
  groundwater plumbing 43, 47
  solar 24, 41–46, 56, 176

H
Harmson, Kim 112–118, 188
Healing Hearts Northwest 117
Hess, Summer 1–8
Hotel Saranac 18, 22, 24, 55, 150
Humaculture 96
Huschke, Kai 5, 131–143

I
The Inlander 166

K
Kizuri 34, 78, 111–114, 116–118, 188, 191
KYRS 18, 26, 88, 89, 91, 93-95, 155, 168. *See also Thin Air Community Radio*

L
LEED 24, 35-37, 46-48, 56
LGBTQ+ 128, 200
Limited Advocacy (program) 68, 69

About the Editor

Summer Hess is an author, social impact advisor with Measure Meant, and the editor of *One-Block Revolution: 20 Years of Community Building*.

Previously, Summer was the managing editor for *Out There Outdoors* magazine, the Inland Northwest's guide to adventure, travel, and outdoor living. Her writing has appeared internationally in *The Spinoff* and nationally in *Writing In and About the Performing and Visual Arts: Creating, Performing, and Teaching*.

Summer has an MFA in writing from Eastern Washington University, where her studies included a year in Chile on a Fulbright fellowship. Her work is informed by a love of mountains and trails and a keen interest in placemaking and civic life. She lives in Wenatchee, Washington with her pack: Matt (partner) and Teako (pup).